DIVE

DEVOTIONS FOR DEEPER LIVING

Cindy Massanari Breeze

Foreword by Michele Hershberger

Library of Congress Cataloging-in-Publication Data

Breeze, Cindy Massanari, 1949-
 Dive : devotions for deeper living / Cindy Massanari Breeze.
   p. cm.
 ISBN 978-0-8361-9615-3 (pbk. : alk. paper) 1. Christian teenagers–Prayers and devotions. I. Title.
 BV4850.B695 2012
 242'.63–dc23

                         2012004175

Dive: Devotions for Deeper Living
Copyright © 2012 by Herald Press, Harrisonburg, Virginia 22802
       Released simultaneously in Canada by Herald Press,
       Waterloo, Ontario N2L 6H7. All rights reserved.
Library of Congress Control Number: 1234567890
International Standard Book Number: 978-0-8361-9615-3
Printed in United States of America
Design by Reuben Graham

Unless otherwise noted, Scripture text is quoted, with permission, from the *New Revised Standard Version*, © 1989, Division of Christian Education of the National Council of Churches of Christ in the United States of America.

Other versions quoted selectively include:
CEV   *Contemporary English Version*
GWT   *God's Word Translation*
KJV   *King James Version*
NKJV   *New King James Version*
NLT   *New Living Translation*

To order or request information, please call 1-800-245-7894 in the U.S. or 1-800-631-6535 in Canada. Or visit www.heraldpress.com.

16 15 14 13 12   11 10 9 8 7 6 5 4 3 2 1

Herald Press
Harrisonburg, Virginia
Waterloo, Ontario

To the youth at First Mennonite Church in Urbana, Illinois,
past, present, and future

TABLE OF CONTENTS

FOREWORD

"Jesus, won't you come by here. Now is the needed time. Oh Jesus, won't you come by here."

When I read these words as part of a story in *Dive*, my heart grew soft. Several thoughts surfaced: Cindy knows how it feels to be in pain. Cindy knows how to tell a story. And Cindy knows Jesus. She's onto something . . . deep.

Not all of the 108 devotions in this book deal with troubled souls. Cindy dives into theological topics such as the nature of God and why bad things happen to good people. She writes of spiritual disciplines such as prayer and service, and about ethical issues such as sexuality or our use of words. There is beauty not only in the diversity of topics but in the push and pull of grace and discipleship. There is the delicate dance of unconditional love with the challenge to grow in faith. The diversity of topics here comes from youth themselves—the participants in Cindy's Sunday school classes over the years. Some subjects aren't surprising, like sex and friendship, but other topics jump out at you—like living out the Lord's Prayer.

I must admit, though, that when I first glanced through the book, I wasn't too excited about reading it. "Oh," I thought, "another set of trite little stories that make it all sound too easy." They remind me of the devotional books I usually got for Christmas when I was in high school.

But I was wrong. The devotions are short, yes, but trite—no. They pack a lot of punch, especially when they tackle subjects like addictions, loving enemies, flawed Bible characters, death, and failure. But it's more than that. Cindy also dares each of us to love ourselves, to gather the courage to claim for ourselves the radical identity of God's beloved daughters and sons. In our day and age, nothing takes more bravery than believing in yourself . . . loving yourself. You know Cindy understands adolescents—and adults, too—when she tells a youth in one of the devotions, "It takes courage to be you." Yes, it does. Yes it does.

It also takes courage to live it out. One of the best parts of this book is the last piece of each section, "Living it out." After they reflect on a subject for several days, Cindy asks youth to do something about it. She calls for such creative things as donating three pieces of *stylish* clothing to a local charity, choosing a "Scripture of hope" to use as a mantra, or interviewing someone about death. This rhythm—reflection and action—actually works in our spiritual growth.

The last several years have yielded major breakthroughs in our understanding Christian youth and how they integrate their faith. Chap Clark, in his book *Hurt*, speaks of today's youth as psychologically abandoned. Parents and other adults spend fewer hours with youth in productive relationship building. And parents ask youth to make agonizing choices, or they exert extreme pressure to succeed, in order to live out the parents' own unfulfilled dreams. Even teens who have loving parents suffer as they live with peers who are more directly abandoned.

With its emphasis on appropriate self-love, *Dive* is one way to address this sense of loneliness and loss. "You are loved," the book whispers. "You are valued."

Another challenge to our spiritual health is the "moral therapeutic deism" religion. In books such as *Soul Searching* by Christian Smith and Melina Lundquist Denton, and *Almost Christian* by Kenda Creasy Dean, we hear about the growing tendency for youth and adults to worship this MTD god who wants us to be nice and feel good, but not necessarily carry our cross or take the teachings of Jesus seriously. Again, *Dive* strives against this false religion, calling us to listen to the biblical God, a God who is still stalking the world today.

Dive: Devotions for Deeper Living is not a cure-all for what ails us. But it is a good resource. It's accessible in its short, easy-reading form that still offers something deeper than the latest self-help cliché. It's authentic, with stories of real people and real pain that dance among the Scripture promises and admonitions. And it takes seriously the ethics—and grace—of Jesus.

"Jesus, won't you come by here. Now is the needed time." Yes, Jesus, in a world of MTD god and abandonment, in a world where it takes courage to be ourselves, in a world of shallow living, we need deep. We need you.

Michele Hershberger, instructor in Bible and Ministry
Hesston College
December, 2011

INTRODUCTION

Before I retired from my work as a pastor, I jokingly asked my youth Sunday school class, "If your parents made you buy and use a devotional book, what topics would you like to see covered?" Collectively they came up with fifty-four topics, and somewhere within these pages, most of their suggestions have been addressed. I trust these will be topics you are interested in as well.

The book is designed for you to use as you wish, at your own pace. You may start at the beginning and work your way straight through or jump from topic to topic depending on your interest. Each devotional entry is anchored in Scripture (*New Revised Standard Version* unless otherwise indicated) and prayer. The last entry in each section is called "Living it out." This may be the most important part of each section, so I hope you don't skip it since each activity will give you an opportunity to make the topic real in your life.

It can be tough being a teenager who tries to follow Jesus. My hope and prayer is that somewhere in these pages you will find encouragement and affirmation for your journey of faith. May you be challenged and strengthened in your relationship with Jesus, knowing how much God loves you.

Cindy Massanari Breeze

001

STRETCHING OUR VIEW OF GOD

Know that the LORD is God. It is he that has made us, and we are his.

« Psalm 100:3

Creator

In the beginning . . . God created the heavens and the earth.
« Genesis 1:1

Have you not known? Have you not heard? The LORD is the everlasting God, the Creator of the ends of the earth.
« Isaiah 40:28

I'm sitting near a window in our cabin in the woods. It is winter in the Midwest, and the landscape is stark. Even so, there are steady reminders of God's creative genius. A squirrel scampers nearby with a giant black walnut in its mouth. The river, partially frozen, reflects the straight, tall trees that will soon burst forth with ash, oak, and hickory leaves. A lone chickadee feasts at a bird feeder, and a cardinal scavenges on the ground for dropped sunflower seeds. A mouse runs across our deck. The sky is blue, the sun is shining, the snow is glistening, and I wonder: even in winter, when we might be tempted to discount the beauty of creation, how could we possibly not celebrate this Creator God who has brought us such a magnificent world?

> *The beauty and mystery of creation draw us into worship and praise of the Creator*

The beauty and mystery of creation draw us into worship and praise of the Creator. Many people say they worship God best in nature. Where are the places you have experienced a closeness to God in creation? Take a minute and think about one of those places. What were your surroundings like? Do you remember any of the sounds of nature? What time of year was it? Was there anyone else with you? How did you feel in this setting? Why do you think the experience made you feel close to God? Can you recapture some of that intimacy with God just by thinking about that experience?

prayer » Creator God, thank you for creating a world of beauty, a place of wholeness. Let me be a steward of this creation. Amen.

Rock

Who is God except the LORD? And who is a Rock besides our God? « Psalm 18:31

I used to live on a street where there was a huge rock on the corner of our block. The rock was a landmark for people trying to find our house, and we'd say, "Just go four houses past the big rock." The rock blocked young children from wandering into the street, and in a neighborhood game of hide-and-seek, it was the place for being "safe." The rock, big and flat, was a favorite spot to rest for a few minutes while on a walk or to eat a picnic lunch. Being on city property, the rock belonged to no one specific, but everyone in the neighborhood thought of it as his or her rock.

If we say someone is a "rock," we understand that this person is steady and strong

If we say someone is a "rock," we understand that this person is steady and strong, someone who can be counted on. When we use the word "rock" to describe God, we imply steadiness and strength as well; it assures us that we can count on God. Other characteristics of rocks also describe God: in existence for a long time, many layered, found everywhere, and good for resting upon.

God is like the rock on our corner: a strong anchor, a place of rest, a safe place, always present, belonging to all.

prayer » **God, I say with the Psalm writer: You alone are my Rock and my salvation. You alone are my Rock of safe refuge. You alone are always present, and in you alone will I put my trust.[1] Amen.**

Shepherd

The LORD is my Shepherd, I shall not want. He makes me lie down in green pastures; he leads me beside still waters; he restores my soul. He leads me in right paths for his name's sake. « Psalm 23:1-3

One of the most familiar names for God in the Bible is Shepherd. Although we no longer live in a time or place where the occupation of shepherd is common, we still understand that when the Bible calls God a Shepherd it is a statement of God's care and comfort. In the well-loved 23rd Psalm, we declare that our Shepherd God will always be with us, will restore our weary souls, and will lead us in the direction we should go.

A good shepherd knows each sheep

Jesus, too, is known as a shepherd. In the Gospel of John he calls himself the Good Shepherd.[2] He reminds the Pharisees—the religious leaders of the day who are continually at odds with Jesus—that a good shepherd knows each sheep by its own individual bleat, and, in turn, each sheep knows its shepherd by the sound of the shepherd's voice. The Pharisees do not realize that Jesus is declaring, as the Good Shepherd, I know all those who follow me by name, and they know me. I love them so much that I would actually lay down my very life for them.

Another time Jesus tells a parable about lost sheep.[3] In this story he says that the Shepherd will leave a flock of ninety-nine sheep alone in the dangers of the wilderness to search high and low for one lost sheep. Jesus is saying that each of us is so important that he will do all he can to bring each one of us "home" to the safety and security of his presence.

prayer » Shepherd God, you give me comfort and keep me safe. You lead me in the way I should go and bring me to a place of peace. Whenever I've lost my way, call me by name and bring me "home." Amen.

Shield

Do not be afraid . . . I am your shield. « Genesis 15:1

I was once at an outdoor party where the winning team of the game we played was given baskets of rotten tomatoes to throw at the losing team. I was a member of the losing team, but fortunately we got shields of metal sheeting to help stave off the messy but fun onslaught.

Shields are for our protection and to ward off danger. Heat shields on spacecraft allow for safe reentry from space. Manufacturers use shields on electronic equipment to reduce unwanted noise. Dentists cover patients with shields when taking X-rays. Baseball catchers wear sun shields on their face-masks in order to see better. Car windshields help keep a driver's vision clear in rain and snow.

God is the shield that keeps us safe and protected from unwelcome danger. In the Psalms we read that God is the shield that saves us.[4] Much more dramatically the Apostle Paul says, "Take the shield of faith, with which you will be able to quench all the flaming arrows of the evil one."[5]

This does not mean that once you are a Christian you will escape all future troubles and trials, that never again will bad things happen to you. You still will face all kinds of hard and unpleasant things in your life, but you do so with God as your Shield—your protection and your confidence.

> *You still will face all kinds of hard and unpleasant things in your life*

prayer » Be my shield, O God, and protect me from the dangers and temptations that seem to be lurking around every corner. In you I put my trust, and in the name of Jesus, I pray. Amen.

Hiding place

You are a hiding place for me. « Psalm 32:7

Ever feel like running away from the hectic pace and pressures of school, home, expectations, and relationships? Ever feel like you could use a week on some secluded island with no one to talk to, no cell phone or computer or iPod—nothing to do but read, sleep, and walk up and down sandy beaches?

There is just such a place, and it is found in God

Many teenagers may cringe at the thought of such relationship and technology withdrawal, but maybe you are one who has longed for a safe place just to be yourself: somewhere you don't have to worry about impressing anyone; somewhere you can safely unload whatever is bothering you; somewhere you can just hide and be loved. There is a safe place, and it is found in God.

You are cordially invited to the Hiding Place.

Where: Anywhere you want it to be

When: Anytime you need it

Why: To take a break from life, spend time with God, and be loved unconditionally

What to bring: Your troubles, cares, anxieties, insecurities, fears, and honesty

No need to RSVP—just show up. God is always waiting for you!

prayer » God, help me remember the ever-present invitation to hide in you and receive your comfort, peace, and love. Amen.

Father and mother

Father of orphans and protector of widows is God in his holy habitation. « Psalm 68:5

As a mother comforts her child, so I will comfort you. « Isaiah 66:13

There is a famous painting by Rembrandt Harmenszoon van Rijn called *Return of the Prodigal Son*.[6] It is an artistic depiction of Jesus' parable[7] where the younger son, after disgracing himself and squandering his inheritance, returns home, destitute and dirty, to the embrace of his father. Rembrandt paints one of the father's hands upon his son's shoulder as strong, muscular, and masculine. The other hand clutching the son is smaller and softer, a more feminine-looking hand.

God wants to love us, care for us, comfort us, correct us, protect us, and guide us

Down through history, people have referred to God as father, but the Bible also presents God with the nurturing characteristics that we frequently associate with mothers. For example, the Psalms tell us that we are safely gathered under the wings of God just like a mother hen gathers her chicks to safety.[8] In the Isaiah verse above, we see that God comforts us as a mother comforts her children.

From Scripture, we learn that God is a like a loving parent, and we are God's children. As our parent, God wants to love us, care for us, comfort us, correct us, protect us, and guide us.

prayer » **Our loving parent, you guide us in the way we should go, and when we let you down, you never stop loving us. Thank you. Amen.**

Living it out

Holy and awesome is [God's] name. « Psalm 111:9

God is Creator, Rock, Shield, Hiding Place, Father and Mother—and so much more. The many names given to God in the Bible help to expand our view of God and stretch our understanding of God. Some of those are given below (the list is neither exhaustive nor in any particular order).

More names for god

Sovereign—Psalm 8:1
Judge—Psalm 50:6; Psalm 96:13; Psalm 98:9
King—Psalm 47:7-8
Deliverer—Psalm 18:2; Psalm 40:17; Psalm 72:12
Redeemer/Savior/Salvation—Psalm 19:14; Psalm 27:1; Psalm 62:2, 6; Psalm 68:19-20; Isaiah 12:2
Most High—Psalm 21:7; Psalm 47:2
Light—Psalm 27:1; John 8:12
Rescuer—Psalm 37:40
Mighty One—Psalm 45:3; Psalm 50:1; Isaiah 60:16
Refuge—Psalm 46:1; Psalm 61:3; Psalm 62:7
Strength—Psalm 118:14; Jeremiah 16:19
Sun—Psalm 84:11
Dwelling Place—Psalm 90:1; Psalm 91:9
Keeper—Psalm 121:5
Almighty—Genesis 17:1; Revelation 1:8; Revelation 15:3

After reading through the list, choose one of the names that is interesting to you.

Questions for reflection

1. Read the biblical passage that corresponds to the name you have chosen to explore. Copy the verse below. (If there are multiple verses given for a name, write down the one you prefer.)

    _____

    _____

    _____

    _____

2. In your own words, rewrite (paraphrase) this passage in words that are more contemporary.

    _____

    _____

    _____

    _____

    _____

    _____

    _____

    _____

3. Is this a name of God that you find helpful? Why or why not?

    _____

    _____

    _____

    _____

4. Using your imagination, what name would you give to God?

    _____

    _____

5. Write a short prayer to God using the name you have chosen.

    _____

    _____

    _____

    _____

    _____

NOTES

1. Psalm 62:2
2. John 10:1-18
3. Luke 15:4-7
4. Psalm 7:10
5. Ephesians 6:16
6. Find the painting at: www.hermitagemuseum.org and search for *Return of the Prodigal Son.*
7. Luke 15:11-32
8. Psalm 36:7 and Psalm 57:1

002
JESUS SAID THAT?

I have come as light into the world, so that everyone who believes in me should not remain in the darkness. « John 12:46

Do not judge

[Jesus said,] "Do not judge and you will not be judged; do not condemn, and you will not be condemned." « Luke 6:37

In the sixth chapter of Luke, Jesus preaches a powerful sermon to a huge crowd of people. (This sermon is sometimes called the Sermon on the Plain.[1]) He delivers a number of rapid-fire directives, including do not judge or condemn others because if you do, you can expect to be judged and condemned yourself.

> *We humans are good at noticing and pointing out the failures in the lives of others while blindly ignoring our own*

I have never thought of myself as being a judgmental person, but as an experiment I decided to keep track of every negative or judgmental thought I had about someone for an entire day. I found myself critical of many people and things. A middle-aged woman wearing a very short skirt—didn't she look in the mirror? A junky yard—were the tenants lazy? Loud and unsupervised children at the grocery store—where was their mother? An email full of misspelled words—didn't the writer know about spell-check? A driver who seemed unaware of turn signals—where did he learn to drive?

I won't embarrass myself with the entire list of condemnations I made, but it is clear that I need to take heed of Jesus' words as much as the next person. Later, in the Sermon on the Plain, Jesus says, "Why do you see the speck in your neighbor's eye, but do not notice the log in your own eye?"[2] We humans are good at noticing and pointing out the failures in the lives of others while blindly ignoring our own shortcomings. I, too, have misspelled words and driven poorly. I surely need to remove my own "logs" before criticizing someone else's "specks."

prayer » God, I don't want to be a judgmental, condemning, critical person. By the power of your Holy Spirit, give me the grace to see others as Jesus sees them. In the name of Jesus, Amen.

Do not get even

[Jesus said,] "You have heard that it was said, 'An eye for an eye and a tooth for a tooth.' But I say to you . . . if anyone strikes you on the right cheek, turn the other also; and if anyone wants to sue you and take your coat, give your cloak as well; and if anyone forces you to go one mile, go also the second mile."
« Matthew 5:38-41

You hit me; I'm going to hit you. You cheated me; I'll cheat you. You said something mean about me; I'll say mean things about you.

Jesus, in the Sermon on the Mount,[3] turns things upside down when he offers a viewpoint opposite of the Old Testament's "eye for eye, tooth for tooth."[4] He radically suggests that we not strike back, not seek revenge, not retaliate. Instead, Jesus expects us to be kind, generous, forgiving, gentle, caring, considerate, and patient—all things counter to getting even.

> *[Jesus] radically suggests that we not strike back, not seek revenge, not retaliate*

This way of acting is as revolutionary today as it was in Jesus' day—and just as difficult. Society's prevailing attitude is that no one is going to take advantage of me. It is so tempting to want to get back and get even, and we need to rely on the strength that Jesus offers in order to rise above the tendency toward revenge. Only with that power can we say, "You hit me, but I will not hit you back! You cheated me, but I have no interest in cheating you. You said something mean about me, but I will not say unkind things about you."

prayer » When I am wronged, God, I want to get even. But I know Jesus is calling me to be generous in spirit and in action. I ask that you give me the desire and the strength to treat others as I would want to be treated. In Jesus' name I pray. Amen.

Age doesn't matter

[Jesus said,] "Truly I tell you, whoever does not receive the kingdom of God as a little child will never enter it." « Mark 10:15

The disciples, trying to protect Jesus from the ever-growing crowds, speak sternly to the parents who are pushing forward so he can touch and bless their children. Jesus becomes irritated with the disciples and says, "Do not keep the little children from coming to me, for the kingdom of God belongs to such as these."

It must have been tough being a disciple. Here they are, trying to protect Jesus and give him some much needed rest from the demanding crowds, and, instead, they end up being scolded. Jesus is trying to teach his followers that children and youth matter. He wants them to know that the simple, trusting faith of young people is the kind of faith all his followers should have. When Jesus gathers the young ones to his knee, he is saying that age has nothing to do with being part of God's kingdom.

The simple, trusting faith of young people is the kind of faith all his followers should have

This little story is found in three of the four Gospels, so we can be sure it is an important one.[5] Whatever your age, you matter to Jesus. Do not question your place in the kingdom of God or underestimate all that you have to offer. The Apostle Paul emphasizes this in a letter to his young friend Timothy, "Let no one despise your youth."[6] Embrace your youthful understanding of the good news of Jesus. Step out into the world knowing that you represent the kingdom of God—even if you don't have all of this faith stuff figured out.

prayer » I think of you gathering the young ones close to your side, and I thank you for gathering me close, too, Jesus. Do not let me be discouraged because of my age. Increase my understanding of your kingdom, and help me be a witness to your goodness and love. In Jesus' name, Amen.

Follow me

[Jesus said,] "Everyone who has left houses or brothers or sisters or father or mother or children or fields, for my name's sake, will receive a hundredfold, and will inherit eternal life."
« Matthew 19:29

Have you ever thought about what the disciples sacrificed to be full-time students of Jesus? They gave up their families, homes, jobs, friends, stability, and comfort. Peter, who must have been feeling homesick for his former life, says to Jesus, "Look, we have left everything and followed you. What then will we have?"[7] I think he probably meant, "Look! We have given up everything for you—what's in it for us?"

Peter is my favorite disciple. He gets in trouble with Jesus quite a bit, but he's refreshingly honest and outspoken. I imagine he says what all the other disciples wish they had the nerve to say. And he has a valid question: What *do* we get out of following Jesus?

What do we get out of following Jesus?

Jesus' answer to Peter is that we can expect eternal life if we follow him. Heaven is a pretty great outcome for following Jesus, but it is an outcome that may be so far into the future that it is difficult to get one's mind around. There must be something in the present that makes it worth following Jesus, right? Each of us has to identify the reasons we choose to be a Christian. Not the reasons our parents or pastor give. Not the reasons we learn about from our youth leader. Our own reasons. Spend the next few days thinking about why you follow Jesus, and you will have an opportunity to record your thoughts in this topic's "Living it out" entry.

prayer » I follow you, Jesus, not just for the reward of life eternal, but also for the joy of right now. I follow you out of love and confidence. I follow you with gratitude and praise. In your name I pray. Amen.

Be real

[Jesus said,] "Beware of practicing your piety before others in order to be seen by them; for then you have no reward from your Father in heaven." « Matthew 6:1

Pretending to be a good Christian to impress others is an empty Christianity

I know someone who is often called upon to pray at public gatherings. He talks frequently about his church attendance and serves on this or that charitable board. From all outward appearances he seems to take his faith seriously, and people praise him for his spirituality and commitment to God. In more private settings, however, I've also seen this man inebriated, speak profanities, and deliver one off-color joke after another. He is definitely one way in public and another way in private.

Jesus warns us about people who play-act at being spiritual. He says that those who are so focused on practicing their piety before others have already received all the reward they are going to get. Pretending to be a good Christian to impress others is an empty Christianity. People who are truly faith-filled and spiritual are humble; they are people who serve God and follow Jesus without needing or seeking the approval or admiration of others.

Be honest. Be yourself. Don't give in to the temptation to act one way in front of your church friends and another way in front of others. Honor both yourself and your commitment to Jesus.

prayer » Lord, I confess that sometimes I want to be seen as some kind of "super Christian." You know and I know that it is a mistake for me to be anything except an honest and humble follower. Bless my attempts at being the kind of person you want me to be. In Jesus' name I pray to you. Amen.

Let your light shine

[Jesus said,] "No one, after lighting a lamp hides it under a jar, or puts in under a bed, but puts it on a lampstand, so that those who enter may see the light." « Luke 8:16

On one hand, Jesus warns us about "practicing our piety before others" so people think we are some kind of "super Christian." On the other hand, today's Scripture seems to contradict that warning since we are advised not to hide the light of Christ away so completely that others do not notice it. Are others supposed to notice that we are Christians or not? Yes and no.

There is a big difference between loudly advertising our own super-religiosity and just letting the way we live announce that we are Jesus followers. But then, if people cannot tell we are Christ followers by the way we live, we might be hiding our relationship with Jesus "under a jar or bed" (as mentioned in the Scripture above).

After my father died, one of his customers wrote me a note and said that she knew my dad was a Christian from the moment they met, long before they ever talked about it. She wrote, "Your father clearly lived out his faith. By his honesty, compassion, kind words, and caring spirit, I just knew he had to be a Christian. His was a quiet witness, but his words and actions were louder than a thousand noisy television preachers."

Following Jesus is good news. And the good news is best when it is shared with others in a sincere way that high-lights Jesus, not ourselves.

What do we get out of following Jesus?

prayer » **God, help me always know the difference between sharing the true Light of Jesus and tooting my own religious horn. I pray in the name of the Light of the World. Amen.**

Living it out

[Jesus said,] "If any want to become my followers, let them deny themselves and take up their cross daily and follow me. « Luke 9:23

Choose one of the following options—or both if you like.

Activity One

Try the same experiment I did earlier in this section. Keep a notebook handy for one whole day and write down everything negative or judgmental you think or say about someone. Look over your list at the end of the day. How judgmental do you think you were? Did your results surprise you? Do you find that if you try to put yourself "in the shoes" of a person, you are less critical?

_____

_____

_____

_____

_____

_____

_____

_____

_____

_____

_____

_____

_____

_____

_____

_____

_____

_____

_____

_____

_____

Activity Two

In the fourth entry in this section ("Follow me"), I asked you to spend a few days thinking about why you choose to follow Jesus. Let's pretend that for some reason you had to defend being a follower of Jesus (and remember in some places and at various times this question was—and still is—more than just a "Living it out" exercise). List any reason you find it compelling to be a Christian, however profound or trivial. Feel free to explain your answers more fully.

WHY I CHOOSE TO FOLLOW JESUS:

_____
_____
_____
_____
_____
_____
_____
_____
_____
_____
_____
_____
_____
_____
_____
_____
_____
_____
_____
_____
_____
_____

Consider sharing your list with a parent, pastor, teacher, youth leader, or friend. Perhaps they will be motivated to create or compare their own list of reasons why they follow Jesus.

NOTES

1. Luke 6:17-49
2. Luke 6:41
3. Matthew 5–7
4. Leviticus 24:20
5. Matthew 19:13-15; Mark 9:33-37; Mark 10:13-16; Luke 18:15-17
6. 1 Timothy 4:12
7. Matthew 19:27-30

003

SPIRIT-FILLED CHRISTIANS

The fruit of the Spirit is love, joy, peace, patience, kindness, generosity, faithfulness, gentleness, and self-control. « Galatians 5:22-23

Joy

Rejoice with an indescribable and glorious joy. « 1 Peter 1:8

Mr. Davidson lived next to the park where we neighborhood children played all summer. Unfortunately, wayward softballs routinely crushed his flowers, and occasionally a baseball crashed through his large front window during an evening Little League game. Mr. Davidson was scary. We would go as a group to retrieve balls, not wanting anyone to experience his anger alone. The minute we stepped into his yard, he would run out the door, yelling and shaking his fist. Once he even chased us out of the yard waving a lead pipe. Now here's the ironic thing: Mr. Davidson had a sign in his yard that said JESUS SAVES and another sign on his front door that said WHERE WILL YOU SPEND ETERNITY?

I am confused by grumpy Christians

I am confused by grumpy Christians. How did Mr. Davidson mesh "Rejoice in the Lord always"[1] with yelling obscenities at children? How would he explain the command to "love your neighbor as yourself"[2] and swinging a lead pipe at those neighbors?

I'm guessing there were significant reasons Mr. Davidson was not filled with joy, and I am sad that the message "Jesus saves" did not put a smile on his face and a song in his heart. I wish Mr. Davidson had been filled with that kind of joy described by the writer of the Psalms: "Sing to the Lord . . . for [God] has done marvelous things. Make a joyful noise to the Lord [and] break forth into joyous song. Let the sea roar, and all that fills it; the world and those who live in it. Let the floods clap their hands; let the hills sing together for joy at the presence of the Lord."[3]

prayer » **With joy I face this day and hope that someone will see Jesus through me. In the name of the one who came to bring "Joy to the World," Amen.**

Patience

You also must be patient. « James 5:8

The Apostle Paul tells us that one of the evidences of a life guided by the Holy Spirit is patience.[4] Gulp!

I'm not sure how much heredity has to do with patience. One of my parents was very patient, the other not so much. Nor do I know how much one's personality determines a person's level of patience. I am pretty sure, however, that many of us could work on being more patient. I speak from personal experience since, for most of my life, I have been trying to become more patient.

On a scale of one to ten, with one being very impatient and ten being very patient, where would you place yourself? If you place yourself above five, congratulations! You have either been given or have developed a valuable tool for life. Your ability to cope with life in healthy and positive ways will serve you well. Thank God for your gift of patience.

If you score below five, here are a few things you could consider. You do not need to remain an impatient person. You can practice patience until it becomes a more natural response. How? Pray for God to fill you with an attitude and spirit of patience. Observe people who you think are patient. What do you learn from your observations? Try counting to ten (or one hundred) before you say or do something driven by impatience—something you later regret. Keep Jesus' Golden Rule in mind when you are tempted to be impatient with someone: "Do to others as you would have them do to you."[5]

Your ability to cope with life in healthy and positive ways will serve you well

prayer » Grant me patience, God, when I have little of my own. Help me see each person and each situation I encounter as blessings, not irritations or inconveniences. Amen.

Kindness

Be kind to one another. « Ephesians 4:32

Kindness and following Jesus go hand in hand

One of the kindest persons I know seems to know innately when someone is in need of a smile, an encouraging word, a hug, a batch of cookies, or a friendly note. And guess what—this person is not an adult. She is a teenager.

Here's what I have learned about kindness from observing her.

- Kind people notice individuals and situations around them and act upon what they notice.
- Kind people focus less on themselves and more on others.
- Kindness is contagious.
- Acts of kindness have a tendency to multiply. The recipient of kindness often pays that kindness forward.
- Sometimes simple acts of kindness have life-changing effects on the recipient. The person who extends that kindness may never know the impact of those kind of actions, but kind people do not extend kindness to reap any rewards.
- Kindness and joy are tightly connected.
- Kindness and following Jesus go hand in hand.

prayer » **Show me today, Lord, where I may extend kindness: in my speech, in my actions, in my attitude. May someone's day be brightened by my kindness. Amen.**

Generosity

Keep this generous spirit alive forever in these people always, keep their hearts set firmly in you. « 1 Chronicles 29:18 (*The Message*)

The word generosity usually refers to being unselfish with one's money and material resources. But it can also mean being generous with one's time. My parents modeled for my brothers and me that part of what we owe God, in addition to our money, is our time. I like the phrase "generous spirit" in our key verse. Having a "generous spirit" opens us up to living lives that are not selfish. If we are generous, we find time to be there for others.

Time is a precious commodity, isn't it? You likely find yourself frequently short on time. There are always papers to write; projects and homework to complete; tests to study for; music to practice; sports to play; extra-curricular activities to participate in; household chores to complete; jobs to get to; people to see; and youth group, church, and parties to attend. Just reading the list makes me want to stop and catch my breath!

One busy time in your life will probably be replaced with another busy time

Maybe you are thinking, I don't have time for a generous spirit right now. I'll just get through high school and things will settle down. Being realistic, however, one busy time in your life will probably be replaced with another busy time. Having a "generous spirit" means that you find ways to carve out time for others and for God despite a busy schedule. It means that you constantly reassess your priorities based on the needs around you.

prayer » **I want to have a generous spirit, God. Help me find the time to be available to the needs around me. Help me keep my "heart set firmly in you" so that those whom I meet may see you through my actions. In the name of the one I follow, Amen.**

Gentleness

Speak evil of no one . . . avoid quarreling . . . be gentle, and . . . show every courtesy to everyone. « Titus 3:2

Jesus says, "Blessed are the meek, for they will inherit the earth."[6] The meek or gentle will inherit the earth? Isn't gentleness a sign of weakness?

Gentle people do not always insist on their own way. Gentle people do not speak in loud and angry ways. Gentle people do not use physical force to solve their problems or express their anger. Gentle people respond to situations in deliberate, well-thought-out ways. Gentle people have a gift for calming situations around them. Are such people weak?

Gentle people have a gift for calming situations around them. Are such people weak?

Mahatma Gandhi immediately comes to mind when I think of gentleness. Recently I toured Birla House in New Delhi, India, where he was assassinated, shot on his way to speak to a large crowd who had gathered on the lawn. Although he was a small, thin, and frail man, there was nothing weak about Gandhi. This soft-spoken and nonviolent man changed the course of history.

Gentleness seems to come more naturally to some than to others. If you have trouble with gentleness, try practicing these three steps toward becoming more gentle:

1. Resist the urge to immediately barge into a situation with your mouth or body.
2. Assess what your role is or is not in the situation.
3. React with gentleness and calmness.

Gentleness is not weakness; it is a strength of character.

prayer » God, help me be a gentle person, always thinking before I speak or act in ways that dishonor you or myself. Amen.

Self-control

A person without self-control is like a house with its doors and windows knocked out. « Proverbs 25:28 (*The Message*)

"Control yourself," your parents probably said when you were younger. They likely meant settle down, lower your voice, quit jumping around, or any number of things children do just because they are children. But you are no longer a little child, so what does self-control mean now?

In a nutshell, self-control is the ability to refrain from what is harmful.

The Apostle Paul lists behaviors that indicate a loss of self-control. These harmful things include "repetitive, loveless, cheap sex; a stinking accumulation of mental and emotional garbage; frenzied and joyless grabs for happiness; trinket gods; magic-show religion; paranoid loneliness; cutthroat competition; all-consuming-yet-never-satisfied wants; a brutal temper; an impotence to love or be loved; divided homes and divided lives; small-minded and lopsided pursuits; the vicious habit of depersonalizing everyone into a rival; uncontrolled and uncontrollable addictions; [and] ugly parodies of community."[7]

Self-control will allow you to focus on behaviors that are nourishing and nurturing

Self-control will allow you to avoid drugs, sex, drinking, driving too fast, pornography, cheating, anger, meanness, jealousy, envy, self-absorption, worship of technology, and nasty language. Self-control will allow you to focus on behaviors that are nourishing and nurturing. Self-control will allow you to be strong with God's help. You can do it! It is for your own health, happiness, and holiness.

prayer » Help me discipline myself to stay away from the temptations everywhere around me. Help me have self-control in everything I say and do. I know it won't always be easy or popular, but with the guidance of the Holy Spirit, I will try. In Jesus' name, Amen.

Living it out

The fruit of the Spirit is love, joy, peace, patience, kindness, generosity, faithfulness, gentleness, and self-control.
« Galatians 5:22-23

In this section, we looked at six characteristics of Spirit-filled Christians:

joy	generosity	patience
gentleness	kindness	control

Looking at the list, put the characteristics in the order you think you are strongest (#1) to the weakest (#6).

1. _____
2. _____
3. _____
4. _____
5. _____
6. _____

Copy the list of six characteristics and give it to someone you trust and know well. Ask them to put the six characteristics in the order they think you are strongest (#1) to weakest (#6).

1. _____
2. _____
3. _____
4. _____
5. _____
6. _____

Compare your list and their list. How similar or different are the lists? Engage the person in a conversation about why they ordered the list the way they did. If you wish, do the same exercise with someone else and then compare the three lists.

Based on the input from yourself and others, what are your two strongest characteristics?

_____

_____

Based on the input from yourself and others, in what area do you need the most growth (your #6)?

_____

_____

_____

_____

_____

Below, make a "game plan" of how you could go about growing in the area that you feel you need to work on the most.

Area that could use growth:

_____

_____

_____

_____

_____

An example of a time when I could have used more of this characteristic:

_____

_____

_____

_____

_____

Three ways that I could work on improvement in this area:

1. _____

2. _____

3. _____

NOTES

1. Philippians 4:4
2. Matthew 22:39
3. Psalm 98:1, 4, 7-8
4. Galatians 5:22
5. Matthew 7:12 and Luke 6:31
6. Matthew 5:5
7. Galatians 5:19-21 (*The Message*)

004
PRAYER CONNECTIONS

This is the boldness we have in [Christ], that if we ask anything according to his will, he hears us. And if we know that he hears us in whatever we ask, we know that we have obtained the requests made of him. « 1 John 5:14-15

Your prayer experience

Be gracious to me, and hear my prayer. « Psalm 4:1

One evening, my younger brother asked if he could pray before dinner. Little did we know that he had just learned the fifty states in alphabetical order. "Thank you, God, for all the people in Alabama. Thank you, God for all the people in Alaska," and state-by-state the whole country was prayed for. My other brother and I, even with our eye rolling and nudges under the table, knew better than to snicker or interrupt the prayer.

Will you be open to new thoughts and experiments?

My family prayed a lot—before meals, during daily family devotions, before bed, and at church on Sundays and Wednesdays. Those early exposures to prayer may have annoyed me at times, but they have given me a great appreciation for the power of prayer.

I know each person has unique experiences or lack of experience with prayer. Over the years youth have shared with me statements like these about prayer:
- I find praying awkward or difficult.
- I only think about praying when I really need something.
- I might pray in church but don't think much about prayer otherwise.
- I am not comfortable praying out loud or in public.
- I need some advice on how to pray.
- I'm not sure prayer really works or makes sense.
- I am willing to explore making prayer a priority in my life, but I don't know how.

Regardless of your previous experiences and thoughts about prayer, will you be open to new thoughts and experiments? Think about it, and then try some of the "experiments" in the next few devotional pieces.

prayer » Help me be open to learning more about prayer. Amen.

A.C.T.S. prayer

In everything by prayer and supplication with thanksgiving let your requests be made known to God. « Philippians 4:6

- God, please let her say yes when I ask her to prom.
- I could use a car, God.
- God, even though I didn't prepare for my audition, please, please, please let me make callbacks for the school musical.
- You know, God, I absolutely have to have a good grade on this algebra test.

I've heard this kind of praying called Santa Claus prayer, and although it is certainly not wrong to ask for things we want or need, we diminish the possibility of an in-depth relationship with God when our prayers focus only on our personal shopping list of desires.

One way to expand our prayer experience is to structure a prayer time using the acronym A.C.T.S.

You know, God, I absolutely have to have a good grade on this algebra test

A—Adoration
Begin with prayers that praise and honor God. This is what Jesus meant when he told us to begin our prayers with "hallowed be your name."[1]

C—Confession
Spend time acknowledging the things you need to confess, asking God for guidance, forgiveness, and grace.

T—Thanksgiving
Thank God for the many blessings in your life, even if you are going through some difficult times.

S—Supplication
This means praying sincerely for others and for yourself. Notice that in the A.C.T.S. prayer, one ends with requests—after praising, thanking, and confessing.

prayer » Holy and great God, I praise you and give you thanks. Amen.

Sentence prayer

Pray without ceasing. « 1 Thessalonians 5:17

Pray without ceasing? Pray 24/7? Perhaps you are thinking, I'll just skip this page and move on. After all, I live in the real world, not in some kind of monastery where praying any time of day or night would seem normal. The Apostle Paul's point of saying that we should pray without ever stopping is not actually to suggest some impossible task, but to encourage us to make prayer a natural part of our lives, day in and day out, minute by minute.

What God does care about is being in communication with us

Keeping ourselves in a constant state of prayer means that we are in frequent conversation with God. Short sentence prayers connect us to God with few words. Simple and honest thoughts expressed in just a sentence— spoken or unspoken. Examples: Thank you for this beautiful day. Help me be kind to this irritable clerk. I don't know what to do!

God cares nothing about how eloquent we are when we pray. God cares little about the length of our prayers or whether we use big words and sound intelligent. What God does care about is being in communication with us. Sentence prayers—quick, to the point, and frequent—are almost like text messages that you send to a friend, only in this case the friend is God.

If sentence prayer is new to you, begin by consciously trying it several times a day. Before long, it might become second nature and something you do without giving it much thought. (My friend calls these "arrow" prayers since she shoots them off to God at any time and place.)

prayer » **Friend God, I need you. I want to be in conversation with you, and I'll try not to worry about my words—just pray from my heart. I know you will hear me. In the name of the one who taught us how to pray, Amen.**

46

Mantra prayer

Hear my prayer, O LORD, and give ear to my cry.
« Psalm 39:12

Throughout the Gospels, Jesus slips away from the disciples and crowds to be alone with God. This has been a powerful lesson for me. If Jesus needed to be renewed and strengthened by relating to God through prayer, then I surely need to pray as well.

"But I don't know what to say when I pray!" you might exclaim. Mantra prayer is an easy and effective way to pray when you have trouble finding words to say, when you are unsure of what to pray for, or when something is so wonderful you do not know how to express your joy. Mantras are short phrases or sentences that are repeated over and over—out loud or silently. These repeated and simple phrases become prayers of the heart.

A teenager came by my office one day with a concern so overwhelming to her that she was nearly speechless. After hearing about her problems, I, too, was nearly speechless and wondered how to even begin praying with her. Earlier that day I had been listening to an African-American spiritual with the words "Jesus, won't you come by here; now is the needed time."[2] As her tears flowed, I began to quietly pray aloud those same words over and over. "Jesus won't you come by here? Jesus, won't you come by here? Jesus, won't you come by here?" Gradually her tears lessened, and she began

These repeated and simple phrases become prayers of the heart

to quietly say with me, "Jesus won't you come by here?" We prayed that mantra for more than ten minutes, and God's peace gradually settled over us both. She left my office with renewed strength for her very difficult times ahead.

prayer » Thank you, God, for the power of simple words. In Jesus' name, Amen.

Intercessory prayer

First of all, I ask you to pray for everyone. Ask God to help and bless them all, and tell God how thankful you are for each of them. « 1 Timothy 2:1 (*CEV*)

One of my friends has made prayer such a priority in her life that she takes a notebook with her everywhere to record people and situations for which she can pray. Every morning after breakfast she opens this notebook and begins an extensive prayer time. And I do mean extensive—sometimes a couple of hours!

In case you are wondering if I am going to suggest this is what you should be doing, relax. Not many of us have the time or the inclination for this kind of prayer life. But from observing my friend's dedication and commitment to prayer I have learned several things:

- Ordinary people can have extraordinary prayer lives.
- I can strive for consistency and regularity in my own prayer life—even if the time I spend in prayer is very short.
- I can make the effort to be observant and mindful of people and situations that need my prayer.
- I can make my prayers more about others and less about myself.
- I can be aware of answered prayer. (My friend keeps track of all answered prayers in her notebook.)

If you are attentive, you will find many, many needs that you could pray about

Praying for others is called intercessory prayer. This type of prayer takes the attention from ourselves and places it on the needs of others. On any given day, if you are attentive, you will find many, many needs that you could pray about. Choose a few of those needs and pray about them in any way you choose. Try this again the next day and the next. After a few days, you will be eager to see what new prayer opportunities come your way.

prayer » Help me pray for the needs of others at least as much as I pray for myself. In Jesus' name, Amen.

Let-others-do-it-for-you prayer

The Spirit helps us in our weakness; for we do not know how to pray as we ought, but that very Spirit intercedes with sighs too deep for words. And God, who searches the heart, knows what is the mind of the Spirit, because the Spirit intercedes for the saints according to the will of God. « Romans 8:26-27

There are times when we are too sad, too upset, too depressed, too confused, too angry, and too despairing to pray. No matter how faithful a Christian we are, there are times when we feel like God has abandoned us or when we simply—for whatever reason—find ourselves unable to talk to God.

Never underestimate the power of prayer— even when you find you cannot or will not pray

For these spiritually dry times, consider trying these two things. First, let the Holy Spirit take your prayer to God. We are promised, in the Scripture above, that the Holy Spirit will intercede on our behalf with deep sighs when we simply are unable to pray. God honors a prayer like this: "I can't pray right now, God. But you know what I need and how I feel, so I'm going to let the Holy Spirit pray for me."

Second, let others step in and pray on your behalf. Our daughter had to undergo serious back surgery requiring an extensive recovery time when she was twelve years old. As difficult as this was for her and our family, it was devastating when we found out she needed to have the rest of her spine fused just two years later. I was angry, sad, confused, and totally unable to pray. Why was this happening? Where was God? Wasn't her first long period of suffering enough? I couldn't talk to God for a long, long time. That's when a whole lot of other people stepped in to pray for her and for our family.

Never underestimate the power of prayer—even when you find you cannot or will not pray. The power of prayer from God's people is mighty!

prayer » Thanks for the Holy Spirit's sighs and for praying friends. Amen.

Living it out

The prayer of the righteous is powerful and effective.
« James 5:16

My father, though a man I only knew as a fine Christian and a great dad, was apparently rather wild in his younger days. After a late night of partying, he returned home close to daybreak. He took off his shoes at the back door and tiptoed down the hall, hoping to sneak by his parents' bedroom without being heard. As he reached their door, he heard a soft voice speaking. He listened for a moment and peeked into the room to see what was going on. There he saw his mother kneeling by the bed and heard her praying: "God, you know Joe's a good boy at heart. But he's on the wrong path, and I'm worried about him. Please help him see that he needs you in his life."

My dad was stunned. Had his mother been on her knees praying all night? How many nights had she been doing this? That night my dad's life changed, and he forever gave the credit for a transformed life to the prayers of his mother.

Prayer can change things, and you don't have to be as old or experienced as my grandmother was when she prayed for my dad. You may think you are too young or too inexperienced to make any difference with your prayers, but God is just waiting for communication with you, caring absolutely nothing about your age or eloquence.

Take a moment and think of one thing that you would like to pray about. It can be a big thing or little thing, a person or a situation, something that concerns you directly or indirectly. Jot down the concern, and develop a "prayer plan" (a tool that you can use to become a more experienced pray-er).

PRAYER PLAN

1. I am going to pray for or about

    _____

    _____

    _____

2. Why am I going to pray for this?

    _____

    _____

    _____

3. The type of prayer I will use is (choose one or more)
    _____ A.C.T.S. prayer _____ Sentence prayer _____ Mantra prayer
    _____ Written prayer (writing a prayer to read to God)
    _____ Combination of prayer types

4. I will commit to praying for this every day for (choose one)
    _____ 3 days _____ 1 week _____ 2 weeks

5. Depending on how many days I've committed to, I will mark off each day I
    pray. 1 2 3 4 5 6 7 8 9 10 11 12 13 14

6. After the time I've committed to is over,
    a. Has anything changed in the situation I prayed for? If so, what?

    _____

    _____

    _____

    b. Have I changed in any way during this "Living it out" prayer plan?

    _____

    _____

    _____

    c. How am I feeling about the role of prayer in my life?

    _____

    _____

    _____

NOTES

1. Matthew 6:9
2. "Needed Time." *American Blues*, with Eric Bibb, Putamayo World Music, PUT215-2, 2003, compact disc.

005
LIVING THE LORD'S PRAYER

Our Father which art in heaven,
Hallowed be thy name.
Thy kingdom come,
Thy will be done in earth, as it is in heaven.
Give us this day our daily bread.
And forgive us our debts, as we forgive our debtors.
And lead us not into temptation,
but deliver us from evil:
For thine is the kingdom, and the power,
and the glory, for ever. Amen.
« Matthew 6:9-13 (*KJV*)

God's hallowed name

Our Father in heaven, hallowed be your name.
« Matthew 6:9

Ascribe to [God] the glory of [God's] name. « Psalm 29:2

The disciples, brand-new and inexperienced followers, ask Jesus to teach them how to pray. Jesus replies with the prayer that Christians worldwide—even two thousand years later—continue to pray. Although the prayer is fairly short, Jesus introduces something profound and expansive.

Recently I was watching a TV drama where the main character found himself in a dangerous situation and began quietly reciting the Lord's Prayer over and over while searching for a way to safety. Many people learn the Lord's Prayer as children and continue to find it an effective and comforting prayer for the rest of their lives. Some people resist the prayer because in many settings the prayer is delivered in such a robotic way that it becomes almost meaningless. Still others, especially those who use the traditional translation, find the prayer's old-fashioned language ("art," "thy," and "thine") distracting and irrelevant. A closer look at the Lord's Prayer verse by verse may reveal the prayer's relevancy with fresh inspiration.

Jesus introduces something profound and expansive

One of those old-fashioned words is right at the beginning of the prayer—"hallowed." The word hallowed means holy, sacred, blessed, and glorious. When Jesus begins this prayer by dwelling for a moment on the holy name of God, he is doing two things: giving honor and respect to God and modeling that our prayers should begin this way as well—especially before launching into a list of things we want or need.

prayer » How great and awesome you are, God! I honor and praise your hallowed name! In Jesus' name, Amen.

God's kingdom and God's will

Your kingdom come. Your will be done on earth as it is in heaven. « Matthew 6:10

I delight to do your will, O my God. « Psalm 40:8

The Message Bible translates the phrase "your kingdom come, your will be done, on earth as it is in heaven" as "reveal who you are. Set the world right; Do what's best—as above, so below." I like the idea of asking God to set the world right, and it is important to think about how I or you could be part of that plan. But what about the "God's will" part of the prayer?

Our willingness to do God's will is never without God's caring promise

Jesus certainly prayed for God's will to be done. When he was in the garden of Gethsemane, facing what he knew was going to be an agonizing death, he prayed to God: Father, if you are willing, please spare me from what is about to happen. But I pray not for my will, but for your will to be done.[1]

When we pray "your will be done," we join with Jesus in saying to God, "I want what you want when you want it." We are relinquishing any attempt to control God—which of course is impossible anyway. Submitting to God's will means that we are dependent, reliant, and obedient. It means that we will be willing to do what God wants us to do and go where God wants us to go.

Scary? Uncertain? Yes, but our willingness to do God's will is never without God's caring promise: "I know the plans I have for you, . . . plans for your welfare and not for harm, to give you a future with hope."[2]

prayer » **How great and awesome you are, God! Reveal who you are and set the world right. Show me how I can be part of your plan to accomplish this. Hallowed be your name. Amen.**

Daily bread

Give us this day our daily bread. « Matthew 6:11

You can be sure that God will take care of everything you need. « Philippians 4:19 (*The Message*)

"Give us this day our daily bread," Jesus prays. Notice that he doesn't ask God for enough steak, mashed potatoes, veggies and dip, hot rolls, fruit salad, and chocolate cake with fudge icing to last a week. He asks simply that our basic needs be met, that we receive what is necessary to sustain us just today.

We are often discontent with what we have

God's provision for our basic needs reminds me of the Old Testament story of the Hebrew people in the wilderness. Having escaped Egyptian captivity with only what food they could carry, they soon became hungry and grumbled to their leader, Moses. He prayed for food, and God miraculously covered the ground every morning with enough manna (a honey and wafer substance) to feed each person. But some were not content with what they needed for daily consumption and tried gathering a surplus. When they collected more than they actually needed, the manna rotted and became worm infested.[3]

We, too, are often discontent with what we have—wanting more than what is really necessary. Jesus is teaching us in this prayer that we are to pray for what we need. The ongoing challenge for me, however, is making a distinction between what I really need and what I think I really need. How about you?

prayer » God, give me today just what I need, and I will be happy and grateful. Or at least I will try to be happy and grateful. Great is your name. Amen.

56

Forgiveness

And forgive us our debts, as we also have forgiven our debtors. « Matthew 6:12

Forgiving one another, as God in Christ has forgiven you. « Ephesians 4:32

This part of the Lord's Prayer is usually recited one of three ways:
- Forgive us our debts, as we forgive our debtors.
- Forgive us our trespasses, as we forgive those who trespass against us.
- Forgive us our sins, as we forgive those who sin against us.

Perhaps we could also paraphrase the verse this way: Forgive us when we do something wrong, just as we forgive those who do something wrong to us.

Jesus packs a lot into this short verse. First, he assumes that we *will* sin. No doubt about that! Second, Jesus is saying that our sins are forgiven. This gift of forgiveness—ours free for the asking and taking—is called "grace" and is one of the miracles of being a Christian. Third, this never-ending reservoir of God's forgiveness seems to be connected to our willingness to forgive others.

One of the most wonderful stories of God's forgiving grace is the tale of John Newton. For many years, Newton, the captain of an English slave trading ship in the 1700s, traveled from Africa to America and the West Indies with his human cargo. Eventually, as Newton began to read his Bible, he saw that what he was doing was wrong—very wrong. He turned his life over to God and for the remainder of his life preached about God's grace—for himself and for everyone else. John Newton is best known for writing the hymn, "Amazing grace" and for tirelessly working toward the abolishment of the British slave trade.[4]

> **Jesus assumes that we will sin. No doubt about that!**

prayer » **Thank you for the gift of grace. Help me accept that gift and extend its healing power to others. In the name of Jesus who taught us how to pray, Amen.**

Temptations

And lead us not into temptation, but deliver us from evil.
« Matthew 6:13 (*KJV*)

What I don't understand about myself is that I decide one way, but then I act another, doing things I absolutely despise.
« Romans 7:15 (*The Message*)

I really like this verse in Romans. It is *so true!* I set out to do a good thing, but I end up doing something wrong. I don't plan on messing up, but I mess up anyway. Why is that? Probably lots of reasons: human nature, peer pressure, selfishness, carelessness, a spirit of experimentation or adventure, self-gratification, or ignorance, just to name a few.

Resisting temptation takes strength, wisdom, and self-control

You know how difficult it is to resist temptation. Every day there are opportunities to be unkind, to gossip, to be dishonest, and to stretch the truth. All you need to do is watch TV, go to the mall, open a magazine, go online, attend a party, or hang out with friends to experience any number of temptations that could lead to doing something wrong. Jesus knows about temptation firsthand, too. In the chapter right before he teaches the Lord's Prayer, he is tempted four times by the evil one (also called Satan, the devil, and tempter).[5]

Years ago there was a comedian named Flip Wilson who was popular for doing outrageous things and then excusing himself by saying, "The devil made me do it!" The evil one is ready, willing, and able to lead us astray. Resisting temptation takes strength, wisdom, and self-control.

prayer » All around me, God, I am being lured to do something I know is wrong. Sometimes I am just not strong enough or secure enough to resist those temptations. Be with me as I try my best to live a life that pleases you and that is safe and healthy for me. In the name of the one who also understands temptation, Amen.

The kingdom, power, and glory

For the kingdom and the power and the glory are yours forever. « Matthew 6:13

Hallelujah! Salvation and glory and power to our God. « Revelation 19:1

Jesus completes the Lord's Prayer as he began—by praising and honoring God. This gives us a wonderful pattern for our own prayer life—to begin and end prayers by acknowledging God's greatness!

When we are little children, our prayers are narrow and self-focused, much like the following prayers I heard from a group of six-year-olds.

Dear God, it would be okay if you had my little sister go live somewhere else and let her bother that family. Amen.

God: I am really, really sorry that I got in trouble this week. But you know everything, so you know it wasn't really my fault. Can you tell my teacher that? Amen.

God: I want a pet, but mommy says "no." I know you can do anything—even change her mind. I'll promise to be very, very good if you just let me have a cat. Amen.

When we are little children, our prayers are narrow and self-focused

When we become more mature pray-ers, we expand our prayers beyond our own concerns to include words of praise and adoration to God for no other reason than Jesus taught us to do just that.

prayer » **Our Father in heaven, hallowed is your name. Yours is the kingdom and the power and the glory forever. Amen.**

Living it out

Our Father which art in heaven,
Hallowed be thy name.
Thy kingdom come,
Thy will be done in earth, as it is in heaven.
Give us this day our daily bread.
And forgive us our debts, as we forgive our debtors.
And lead us not into temptation,
but deliver us from evil:
For thine is the kingdom, and the power,
and the glory, for ever. Amen.
« Matthew 6:9-13 (*KJV*)

A paraphrase is when something is rewritten in order to make it more current, personal, or easier to understand. When Scripture is paraphrased it is never intended to totally replace the biblical text. However, spending the time it takes to rewrite a passage in our own words often results in a new familiarity, understanding, and appreciation of that Scripture.

Try writing your own paraphrase of the Lord's Prayer in words that are meaningful to you. Before you begin, it might be helpful to read a sample paraphrase of the first verse of the Lord's Prayer:

Awesome, God! You have a holy and special name. I praise and honor you.

Now it is your turn to rewrite the prayer:

My Paraphrase of the Lord's Prayer

Matthew 6:9-13

_____

_____

_____

_____

_____

_____

_____

_____

_____

_____

_____

_____

_____

_____

_____

_____

_____

_____

_____

_____

_____

_____

When completed, take a few moments to pray both the original Lord's Prayer in Matthew and your new, personal version.

NOTES

1. Luke 22:42
2. Jeremiah 29:11
3. Exodus 16
4. Kenneth W. Osbeck, _101 Hymn Stories_ (Grand Rapids: Kregel Publications, 1982) 28-33.
5. Matthew 4:1-11

006

I AM SOMEBODY WORTHWHILE

Are not five sparrows sold for two pennies? Yet not one of them is forgotten in God's sight. But even the hairs of your head are all counted. Do not be afraid; you are of more value than many sparrows. « Luke 12:6-7

God loves me

If God is for us, who is against us? « Romans 8:31

Imagine this scenario: It is the championship game with one second left on the clock. The girl launches a shot, and the ball swishes through the net. The game is won! From the stands the girl's mother yells, "Way to go—you are awesome!" Now imagine this alternative scenario: It is the championship game with one second left on the clock. The girl launches a shot, and the ball bounces on the rim and out of bounds. The game is lost! From the stands the girl's mother yells, "That's okay—you are awesome!"

When we feel unloved, it is easy to slip into feelings of worthlessness

In either scenario, regardless of how her daughter performs, the mother is encouraging, kind, and supportive. God is like this parent—always on our side. We don't need to make a winning basket or do anything else to be loved by God. It is love entirely unearned and not dependent on stellar grades, popularity, good looks, family pedigree, personal wealth, moral living, or anything we do or say. Furthermore, the news gets even better. The Apostle Paul reminds us that there is absolutely nothing that can ever separate us from God's love: not death, not life, not any person, not anything in heaven, not anything on earth, not anything in the past, present, or future.[1]

But why emphasize God's love in a chapter about self-worth? Because when we feel unloved, it is easy to slip into feelings of worthlessness. In God's sight we are anything but worthless. God's acceptance and love for us remain steady, consistent, trustworthy, and unfailing. "If God is for us, who is against us?"

prayer » **God, thank you for your ever-ready and ever-present love. Amen.**

I'm allowed to love myself

God loves you and has chosen you. « Colossians 3:12 (*CEV*)

One morning, just as we were about to wind up our discussion, a youth in my Sunday school class quietly asked, "What are you supposed to do when you don't like yourself very much?" The discussion abruptly halted. Such a vulnerable and courageous remark. Almost every teen in the room, after some initial shyness, responded that from time to time they resonated with the girl's question. The dismissal bell was disregarded, and I put a sign on the door that read, IMPORTANT DISCUSSION GOING ON. WE'LL BE DONE SOON.

I gave all class members a note card and asked them to make a list of all the things they didn't like about themselves. I collected the cards from the youth who didn't mind my reading their list aloud (no names, of course). Their lists included the following reasons: I'm not very smart; I'm too smart; I don't dress right; I don't have enough money to fit in; I'm no good at sports; I'm ugly; my family embarrasses me; I'm a coward and can't stick up for myself; I have really bad acne; I don't know how to act cool around girls; no boy ever gives me a second look.

God creates nothing inferior and that includes you

Almost all teenagers struggle with negative feelings of self-worth, sometimes feeling socially, intellectually, artistically, athletically, and financially inferior to their peers. Maybe it helps to know that even the most attractive, the most athletic, and the most intelligent of your peers probably feel that way sometimes, too. Remember that our self-worth can never be determined by society's external and elusive standards of what makes a person worthwhile. Focus simply on this: God creates nothing inferior and that includes *you*.

prayer » God, help me love myself—just as I am. Amen.

I'm no loser

A voice came from heaven, You are my Son, the Beloved; with you I am well pleased. « Mark 1:11

Early one winter morning I set out from my house in Illinois to drive four hours for the first session of a seminary class in Indiana. Before too many miles, I realized I needed gas. I was irritated with myself for not having planned ahead because even a short delay at the gas station could make me late for class.

> **How could I have been so dense, so unorganized? Why was I such a loser?**

Not a good way to impress a professor! Two hours later I drove into a blinding snowstorm and, now going thirty miles per hour, I wondered why I hadn't checked the forecast. I rummaged inside my purse for my phone to call the seminary receptionist so she could let the professor know I would be a little late. Oh no—my phone was still recharging on the counter at home. I began to mumble about how foolish it was to set out on a trip needing gas, without checking the forecast, and leaving my phone at home. Could I be any more inept? Yes. When a DJ on an Indiana radio station gave the current time, I realized Indiana was one hour ahead of Illinois. How could I have been so dense, so unorganized? Why was I such a loser?

Eventually I arrived on campus and entered the classroom just as the professor was dismissing the class with a blessing. With an inviting smile, she gestured for me to join the circle of students as she recited from the Gospel of Mark: "A voice came from heaven: You are my Son, the beloved; with you I am well pleased." She went to each person in the circle and repeated, "You are the beloved son (or daughter) of God." When she reached me, she said, "Cindy, you are God's beloved daughter, and with you God is well pleased." Then she smiled and added, "even if you did miss my entire first class." With the reminder of God's love, I felt the tension and self-loathing melt away. God found me loveable, despite how inept I had been that morning—or any other morning. If God loves me, I can love me.

prayer » Thank you for loving me so much that you call me your beloved child. In the name of your own beloved Child, Amen.

God don't make no junk!

You are the one who put me together inside my mother's body, and I praise you because of the wonderful way you created me. Everything you do is marvelous.
« Psalm 139:13-14 (*CEV*)

I once saw this on a bumper sticker: *I am somebody because God don't make no junk!* Even with its imperfect grammar, I love that bumper sticker for, in a few well-chosen words it preaches an entire sermon.

For all her life, my friend has endured pesky physical and mental health problems. The more she struggled with her issues, the more she began to lose faith in God and one day asked, "Do you think God has it out for me, or do you think God just goofed up when I was made? Do you think I'm a mistake?" Perhaps you have even wondered the same things.

> *The more she struggled with her issues, the more she began to lose faith*

The only way I could think of to answer my friend's heartfelt and difficult questions was to quote two Scriptures: "God is the one who put you together, and everything God does is marvelous;" (see passage above) and from 1 John, "See what love the Father has given us, that we should be called children of God."[2] I asked her if she thought God, who created us and calls us children, would create junk? She hesitated, so I said, "Of course not; you are somebody because God don't make no junk!" She began to laugh, and once she stopped laughing, she admitted that was true—she was not junk.

My friend's life is still full of challenges, and every once in awhile (just like the rest of us), she again questions God and doubts her self-worth. When I hear her express those feelings, I just look at her with a very somber and serious expression and say, "God don't make no junk!" She smiles or laughs every time.

prayer » **God, thank you for not creating junk. Amen.**

I am more than my abilities

When I thought, "My foot is slipping," your steadfast love, O LORD, held me up. « Psalm 94:18

In high school I was privileged to have leads in musicals, sing solos at assemblies, and participate in many ensembles. I was section leader of the top choir for several years and was given the "outstanding vocal award" my senior year.

My self-worth had nothing to do with my talents or intellect

After high school, I attended a small Christian college to major in music education and minor in voice and choral conducting. Freshman majors were given many wonderful performance opportunities, and once again I sang in the top choir and performed often. I attended that college for only one year because I knew it was a huge sacrifice for my parents to send me to a private institution. Having been awarded a full teacher's scholarship at one of our state universities, I transferred and continued there through graduation. Where before—in high school and during my freshman year of college—I had often been singled out for countless prestigious performance opportunities, that was no longer the case. Everywhere I turned there were better singers than I. I could work and study hard, which I did, but there were *always* many more talented and successful musicians than I would ever be.

This was a major turning point in my life. My self-esteem plummeted. Falling from the top of the musical heap was a humbling experience. But you know what? In retrospect, I think it was one of the best things to ever happen to me. For the first time I realized my self-worth was not dependent on my ability to sing, conduct, or act well. My self-worth had nothing to do with my talents or intellect. I was—and still am—a worthwhile person just because I have been created and loved by God.

prayer » For the gifts and talents I have, I am grateful, God, but I know they don't define me. Thank you loving me just as I am. Amen.

Celebrate the inward and outward you

The LORD said, [People] look at the outward appearance, but the LORD looks at the heart. « 1 Samuel 16:7 (*NIV*)

Between bites of pizza, the group of teens laughed and joked with each other, and from all outward appearances they seemed carefree, happy, and well adjusted. Alicia, though, was trying to look like the models in the latest issue of her favorite teen magazine and had recently begun purging in order to keep her weight under control.

Ross loudly boasted that he was absolutely sure he'd get a football scholarship to any college he wanted to go to, but in reality he wasn't sure about that at all. Maybe last night's touchdowns were just luck.

Manuel kept the group entertained with one joke after another. He thought he was doing a good job of convincing the others that he was happy, but inside he felt so sad, such a nobody.

Turn those self-doubts over to God

Gina looked around the table at her friends and wished she could be as pretty as Alicia and Rosa, as rich as Matthew, as smart as Jessica, and as funny as Manuel. She was so average, nothing special.

Matthew threw two twenty-dollar bills on the table to pay for the pizza and soda. The others, so used to his paying for everything, barely noticed. He wondered if they would even want to be his friends if he didn't have money.

You probably know from personal experience that outward appearances are not always an indicator of what is going on inside. Whatever struggles you sometimes have with self-esteem, you are in good company—the company of almost every other youth. Turn those self-doubts over to God. Celebrate all that makes you unique and special inside and out. Celebrate *you*!

prayer » God, thank you for being a safe place to be myself. Thank you for knowing my heart. Amen.

Living it out

For we are God's masterpiece. « Ephesians 2:10 (*NLT*)

I Am Somebody
BY JESSE JACKSON

I am Somebody!
I am Somebody!
I may be poor,
But I am Somebody.
I may be young,
But I am Somebody.
I may be on welfare,
But I am Somebody.
I may be small,
But I am Somebody.
I may have made mistakes,
But I am Somebody.
My clothes are different,
My face is different,
My hair is different,
But I am Somebody.
I am black, brown, or white.
I speak a different language
But I must be respected,
Protected,
Never rejected.
I am God's child![3]

This powerful poem, made famous by the Reverend Jesse Jackson, an African-American civil rights advocate, is a testimony to self-worth. Personalize the poem by filling in your own words on the blank lines.

I Am Somebody
BY JESSE JACKSON AND _____

(add your name)

I am Somebody!

I am Somebody!

I may be _____,

But I am Somebody.

I may be _____,

But I am Somebody.

I may be _____,

But I am Somebody

I may be _____,

But I am Somebody.

I may have made mistakes,

But I am Somebody

My _____ is different,

My _____ is different,

My _____ is different,

But I am Somebody.

I am _____, _____, or _____

I _____,

But I must be respected,

Protected,

Never rejected. I am God's child!

NOTES

1. Romans 8:38-39
2. 1 John 3:1
3. Jackson's poem, popularly available on the Internet, is based on a poem of the same name by William H. Borders, quoted in *Sesame Street Unpaved*, by David Borgenicht, (New York: Hyperion Books, 1998), 164.

007
FRIENDSHIP

No one has greater love than this, to lay down one's life for one's friends

« John 15:13

Friends are a great gift

Friends come and friends go, but a true friend sticks by you like family. « Proverbs 18:24 (*The Message*)

You've likely discovered that as you've grown in independence, friendships have increased in importance. Whether you prefer a large group of friends or just one or two close friends, your friends may have become nearly as supportive and influential as your family. Perhaps you choose friend time over family time and have discovered that it is often easier to share more personally and intimately with your friends than with your family.

It is often easier to share more personally and intimately with your friends than with your family

Many parents do not understand this shift in their children. Just a few weeks ago, for example, a mother said to me, "My son spent the entire afternoon with a friend, and five minutes after coming home, he's texting him about something. Why won't he talk to me that much?" I think her question was rhetorical, but I couldn't resist answering. Here's a summary of our conversation.

> **Me:** Is your son's friend a nice person?
> **Mother:** Yes, he is a very nice person.
> **Me:** Does your son ever get into trouble while with this friend?
> **Mother:** Never! I can totally trust the two of them.
> **Me:** Do you think your son would be happier without this friend in his life?
> **Mother:** No, of course not!
> **Me:** Do you realize how fortunate your son is to have found a friend you like and who makes him happy?
> **Mother** (*hesitantly*)**:** Well . . . yes, but I just want things to be like they used to be, you know, where he confides in me and needs me.
> **Me:** He still needs you—but he needs his friends, too.

prayer » Thank you, God, for my friends. Not that they ever replace my family, but for the joy, support, and understanding they add to my life, I give you thanks. In the name of Jesus, Amen.

What makes a good friend?

If you fall, your friend can help you up. But if you fall without having a friend nearby, you are really in trouble. « Ecclesiastes 4:10 (*CEV*)

How do you identify a good friendship? What makes a good friend? You likely have a variety of answers to these two questions, and what you look for in a good friend may be different than what another person may be looking for. I asked six teenagers to tell me what characteristics make a good friend. They said a good friend

How do you identify a good friendship?

- is someone who is willing to listen to everything you have to say without judgment or bias;
- gives modest and gentle advice;
- is aware of how you feel without even asking;
- offers comfort and support;
- shares your pain and grief;
- is easy to talk to;
- is trustworthy, honest, and selfless;
- can tell you when you do something wrong, if something does not look good on you, and when you have spinach in your teeth;
- always wants the best for you;
- is never deliberately mean to you;
- is someone with whom you can totally be yourself. A friend accepts you when you are sad, happy, cranky, or silly;
- does not judge you;
- is fun to be with;
- can be someone just like you or someone very different (either one has its advantages);
- understands the importance of faith in your life.

prayer » **Thank you, God, for good friends. Amen.**

I am a good friend because ...

A friend loves at all times. « Proverbs 17:17

Are you fun to be with?

Understanding what makes someone a good friend is important, but so is examining what makes you a good friend. How would you answer the following questions?

- Are you a good and careful listener?
- Do you try to lift the spirits of friends who are sad or troubled?
- Do you respect the opinions of your friend, even when you totally disagree?
- Can your friend safely share inner feelings with you, and can you be trusted with confidentiality?
- Do you try to give serious, reliable, and well-thought-out advice when a friend seeks you out with a problem?
- Do you judge your friend?
- Are you jealous of your friend? Envious?
- Are you committed to working out problems that arise with a friend? In other words, are you committed enough to the relationship to weather the stormy times?
- Do you need to be the center of attention in the friendship? Does the friendship have to be "all about you"?
- Are you fun to be with?

How do you rate yourself as a friend? Are there areas you need to work on?

prayer » I know it is important for me to know what it takes to be a good friend if I want to have a good friend. If there are areas I need to work on, please help me have the desire and courage to do so. In the name of Jesus, Amen.

Friends are to honor and love

Be devoted to one another in . . . love. Honor one another above yourselves. « Romans 12:10 (*NIV*)

The Bible offers several good examples of friendship: Elijah and Elisha, David and Jonathan, Paul and Timothy, Jesus and his disciples are just a few. One of the best stories is of Ruth and Naomi.[1] Ruth and Naomi live in the country of Moab, just east of Naomi's homeland, Judah. Ruth was married to Naomi's son, and when her husband and Naomi's husband die, the women are grief-stricken and destitute. Naomi decides to return to Judah where she hopes her relatives will take care of her. As she says a tearful goodbye to Ruth and another daughter-in-law, Orpah, Ruth clings to Naomi and says these heartfelt words:

Where you go, I will go; where you live, I will live

> Do not press me to leave you or to turn from following you.
> Where you go, I will go; where you live, I will live.
> Your people will be my people and your God will be my God.
> Where you die, I will die.

Naomi, understanding that Ruth will not be persuaded otherwise, accepts the friendship of her daughter-in-law and settles with her in Bethlehem. Together the two friends overcome poverty and unhappiness. Ruth eventually marries Boaz, one of Naomi's relatives, and when their son Obed is born, the friends of Naomi gather to admire the new baby. They tell her how fortunate she is to have a daughter-in-law who loves her so much and is more precious than seven sons.

The long friendship of Ruth and Naomi is built on love, loyalty, shared experiences, dedication, commitment, generosity, dependence, and joy—characteristics we can all hope for in our friendships.

prayer » **May I be a good friend like Ruth was to Naomi. May I be loyal and kind, generous and loving. In Jesus' name, Amen.**

Friends can let you down

So, could you not stay awake with me one hour?
« Matthew 26:40

Over the piano in my childhood home hung my grandfather's picture of Jesus praying in the garden of Gethsemane on the night he is arrested by religious leaders. In the painting, Jesus is leaning on a large rock in the foreground and at some distance to the far right are the three sleeping figures of his friends.

After the Passover meal where Jesus announces his imminent death, he asks three of his disciples—Peter, James, and John—to go with him to pray in the garden of Gethsemane. "Sit here while I go over there and pray," he says, but the friends are tired, and they soon fall asleep. Jesus returns to them and is distraught to find them sleeping. "So, could you not stay awake with me one hour?" he asks. They feel guilty and are determined to stay awake to support their teacher and friend in prayer, but once again they fall asleep. A second time, Jesus returns and finds them asleep, and again a third time. Clearly disappointed and feeling let down by his closest friends, Jesus says, "Are you still sleeping and taking your rest? See, the hour is at hand, and the Son of Man is betrayed into the hands of sinners. . . . See, my betrayer is at hand."[2]

Even our best friends will disappoint us

I still have Grandpa's picture of Jesus in the garden, and it has brought me to tears more than once. At the very time when Jesus most needed his friends, they let him down—three times! Instead of offering their moral and prayer support, they fell asleep. The reality is that friends let us down. From time to time, due to many circumstances, even our best friends will disappoint us. We will wonder as Jesus did, So you could not come through for me?

prayer » Let me encourage and support my friends when they need me most, and help me forgive them when they let me down. Amen.

Friendship can be repaired

Be gentle with one another, sensitive. Forgive one another as quickly and thoroughly as God in Christ forgave you. « Ephesians 4:32 (*The Message*)

Friends will occasionally disappoint us and, unfortunately, we will occasionally disappoint our friends. When this happens, it is painful. When friends say or do things that are unkind, it hurts. And the closer the friend, the more it hurts. Rifts in friendships require swift action in order for the friendship to stay viable. Several youth shared the following observations with me about their bumpy times with friends:

- "If a friendship is worth having, it is worth fixing things between us when something happens."
- "The quicker the argument or misunderstanding is over between friends, the better."
- "When a friend lets me down, I think it is important to understand why they did what they did."
- "I don't want to lose a friend, so I'll go the second mile to make it work. I hope they do the same with me."
- "I very much want to quickly make amends with my friends."

The words in the focus Scripture above give us helpful advice when dealing with conflict between friends. Be gentle; be sensitive; and forgive quickly—just as Jesus forgives. Besides these qualities, three other tools help repair relationships: honesty, understanding, and compassion.

Be gentle; be sensitive; and forgive quickly

Sometimes the repair process is quick and easy (thank God for that), and sometimes it is long and difficult (ask God for guidance). But whatever time it takes, and however hard it may be, friendship repair is worth it.

prayer » Let me heal my conflicts with gentleness, sensitivity, forgiveness, honesty, understanding, and compassion. In Jesus' name I pray for guidance. Amen.

Living it out

Do not forsake your friend. « Proverbs 27:10

Coming home from work late one evening, I was tired and dreading having to scrounge up something for dinner. I had been so busy that week that I hadn't been able to get to the store. I was pretty sure the menu would include a fried egg or grilled cheese sandwich—again. As I pulled into my driveway, I saw a cooler sitting by the front door. Inside was a large bowl of chicken salad, home-made rolls, green salad, strawberry pie, and a note: "I know it has been a busy and hard week for you. Enjoy dinner and get some rest. Love, ____." That's a good friend!

Frank Dempster Sherman, an American poet who lived from 1860-1916, wrote the following prayer about the joy of friendship. It might be an old, old poem, but the message is still a good one.

> It is my joy in life to find
> At every turning of the road
> The strong arm of a comrade kind
> To help me onward with my load.
>
> And since I have no gold to give,
> And love alone must make amends,
> My only prayer is, while I live—
> God make me worthy of my friends.[3]

All too frequently we take our friends for granted. Or maybe more than taking them for granted, we don't express our gratitude and thanks for their friendship as often as we could. Take this opportunity to do one of the following projects for one (or more) of your friends, something that will say loud and clear how much they mean to you.

1. Write a letter to your friend outlining the things you appreciate about her. Be specific and give examples of times when you have been grateful for something she said or did. If a letter seems too formal or difficult, make a card or write a "Top Ten Things I Appreciate about You" list.

2. Make a batch of your friend's favorite kind of cookies and find an unexpected and creative way to deliver the treat to him.

3. Take some silly photos of you and your friend and put them in a small photo album. You might make a title page that says "Reasons I Like Hanging around with You."

4. "Kidnap" your friend and take him to his favorite restaurant.

5. Pay attention to your friend's favorite songs and make a CD of them for her.

6. Instead of choosing one of the above suggestions, make up your own surprise "thank you for your friendship" activity.

NOTES

1. Ruth 1–4
2. Matthew 26:36-46
3. Charles L. Wallis, ed., *The Treasure Chest* (New York: Harper and Row, 1965), 99.

008
FORGIVENESS

If we confess our sins, [God] who is faithful and just, will forgive us our sins and cleanse us from all unrighteousness. « 1 John 1:9

God forgives

You are a God ready to forgive, gracious and merciful, slow to anger and abounding in steadfast love. « Nehemiah 9:17

Forgiveness is one of those words that you don't usually hear as you walk down the hall between classes. In fact, when was the last time you even heard the word outside of church?

> *God is ready and waiting to "wipe the slate clean"*

One of the things I like best about the Bible is that the characters we read about in its pages are sometimes seriously flawed—kind of like us. They continually mess up. Really mess up! But we don't need to explore Scripture very long before we see that in God's mercy they are offered forgiveness and given second or third (or more) chances to change their ways.

One of the best stories of forgiveness is about King David. He becomes enamored with a married woman named Bathsheba and then sends her husband, Uriah, into the front line of battle hoping he will be killed. Sure enough, that is what happens, and David marries the widow.[1]

There are the stories of Sarah, who laughs at and lies to God's angels;[2] Moses, who kills a man;[3] Delilah, who deceives Samson;[4] and Jonah, who runs away from God.[5] There is the story of Saul/Paul, the fanatic who violently persecutes the followers of Jesus.[6] God lavishes forgiveness on each of them and gives them a chance to make a fresh start.

If God forgives the sins of David, Sarah, Moses, Delilah, Jonah, and Saul, you can be confidant that God will also forgive you. God is ready and waiting to "wipe the slate clean" no matter what you've done. All you have to do is ask.

prayer » God, I try not to mess up, but over and over again I do. So over and over again I ask for your compassion, understanding, and forgiveness. Thank you for the gift of forgiveness that sets things right. Amen.

We can forgive because God does

If you do not forgive others, neither will your Father forgive [you]. « Matthew 6:15

All you have to do to receive God's forgiveness is to ask for it. But it also appears that the measure of forgiveness we experience depends on how much we are willing to forgive others.

Jesus tells the story about a servant who owes his master a lot of money—perhaps as much as several million dollars. The master demands that the servant pay without further delay or he, his entire family, and all his possessions will be sold to help pay the debt. The servant begs and pleads with the master, asking him to reconsider and have compassion for his situation. The master, taking pity on the servant, generously forgives the entire sum and sends him on his way debt-free.

Immediately on leaving the master's mansion, the servant meets a friend who owes him a very small amount of money. He grabs his friend by the neck and demands he instantly repay the money. The friend begs and pleads, asking him to reconsider and have compassion for his situation. But the servant is unforgiving and has the man arrested and thrown into debtor's prison. When the master hears what the servant has done—immediately after the servant's own very large debt has been forgiven—he is very angry. The servant is arrested and sent to prison, too.[7]

If God is so willing to forgive us, how can we possibly deny forgiveness to others?

If God is so willing to forgive us, how can we possibly deny forgiveness to others?

prayer » God, please give me the desire and strength to offer the gift of forgiveness to others as you have so freely given it to me. In Jesus' name, Amen.

Forgiveness can't wait

Be kind to one another, tenderhearted, forgiving one another, as God in Christ has forgiven you. « Ephesians 4:32

Not forgiving someone can really eat you up inside. You probably know that horrible "pit in the stomach" feeling when something just isn't right between you and someone else. Not addressing that "pit" is like ignoring a small splinter in your finger until it festers and works itself into a full-blown infection requiring major intervention to get it under control.

If you don't take care of it soon, it will fester

Attend to what and who needs forgiveness in your life. Don't wait any longer. I can almost guarantee that if you don't take care of it soon, it will fester and work itself into a full-blown infection of your spirit.

Here are several amazing things about forgiveness:
- Asking for forgiveness or extending forgiveness almost immediately gets rid of the "pit in the stomach."
- It is great when someone who has harmed you apologizes and asks for your forgiveness. But even if that does not happen, you can refuse to hold on to that hurt and with God's help forgive that person.
- Being angry, hurt, or filled with hatred toward someone takes more energy than forgiving that person.
- The person who benefits most from a forgiving spirit is the one who forgives.

prayer » I don't want that "pit in the stomach" feeling anymore, God. Help me find the courage to develop a forgiving spirit. I know I can't do it alone. Amen.

Forgiveness is a choice

Forgive us our sins, just as we have forgiven those who sin against us. « Matthew 6:12 (*NLT*)

Corrie ten Boom and her sister were sent to the Ravensbruck concentration camp in Germany during World War II for hiding Jews in their Dutch home. While there, Corrie experienced the death of her sister and witnessed horrific and inhumane atrocities by Nazi soldiers, especially by one officer who made the women parade nude in front of him. Years later, after speaking to an audience about how her faith sustained her during the war, that same officer approached Corrie. He told her that he had recently become a Christian and was grateful for her message that evening. Ten Boom wrote:

You hold the power to extend or accept forgiveness—or not

> His hand was thrust out to shake mine. And I, who had preached so often the need to forgive, kept my hand at my side. "Lord Jesus," I prayed, "forgive me and help me to forgive him." I tried to smile. I struggled to raise my hand. I could not. I breathed a silent prayer. "Jesus, I cannot forgive him. Give me your forgiveness." As I took his hand the most incredible thing happened. From my shoulder along my arm and through my hand a current seemed to pass from me to him, while into my heart sprang a love for this stranger that almost overwhelmed me.[8]

Forgiving someone is a choice. With God's help, you hold the power to extend or accept forgiveness—or not.

prayer » God, the world says "an eye for an eye." To tell you the truth, sometimes that mindset appeals to me. I ask for the grace to crowd out what the world says in order to choose what you say to do, that is, to forgive. In the name of our forgiving Lord, Amen.

Forgiveness again and again

Peter said to Jesus, "Lord, . . . how often should I forgive? As many as seven times?" Jesus said to him, "Not seven times, but, I tell you, seventy-seven times."
« Matthew 18:21-22

Forgiveness is time consuming and rarely a one-time event. It would be nice if we could quickly forgive someone and declare "that's that." Sometimes it may work out that way, but not always. Jesus tells his disciple Peter to be prepared to forgive someone seventy-seven times. Seriously? Seventy-seven times?

A friend of mine once did something that really, really hurt me. That was bad enough, but then she lied about what she had done. I felt betrayed and angry. Eventually I gathered my courage and told her how much she had hurt me. She genuinely asked for my forgiveness, and I accepted her apology. But that initial forgiveness was only the first of many times when I had to make the effort to forgive her. Since we saw each other frequently, I had to consciously forgive her over and over again—perhaps seventy-seven times.

I felt betrayed and angry

I admit that sometimes I didn't want to forgive her because I wasn't sure she had suffered enough for hurting me so badly. I finally realized I couldn't fully forgive her all on my own. Extending forgiveness took a lot of prayer. I am happy to report that eventually my hurt feelings dwindled and disappeared—a sure sign of God's grace.

prayer » God, I wish forgiveness was always just a one-time thing—over and done with. But when it isn't, help me create a space in my heart to offer genuine forgiveness as often as I need to. In the name of the forgiving Jesus, Amen.

Don't believe everything you hear about forgiveness

Forgive each other; just as the Lord has forgiven you, so you also must forgive. « Colossians 3:13

Forgiveness means something different to each of us and is often given or received in a hurried and flip manner. Further, some people think that forgiveness immediately sweeps away any conflict. Here are four common myths about forgiveness:

Forgiveness is necessary . . . but it almost never is easy

1. **Forgiveness means forgetting.** You've probably heard the expression "forgive and forget." The fact is, we can't turn off our brains like some television show we don't like. Could Corrie ten Boom possibly forget about what happened to her sister and her in the concentration camp? Of course not. Forgiving does not depend on forgetting.
2. **Once you've forgiven someone or they have forgiven you, you'll now be good friends.** That might happen, especially with deliberate hard work, but reconciliation does not always result in best-friend status.
3. **Saying "I'm sorry" is a sign of weakness.** Don't be afraid to utter those powerful words as often as necessary—to God and to others. Saying "I'm sorry" is the very foundation of forgiveness and a sign of humility and maturity.
4. **Forgiveness is easy if you are a Christian.** Forgiveness is necessary for a Christian if we take Jesus seriously, but it almost never is easy, comfortable, or quick.

prayer » Give me the desire to forgive—even if I can't always forget. Guide me in loving those whom I have hurt or who have hurt me. Help me say "I'm sorry" often. Give me the courage to forgive, even when it isn't easy, comfortable, or quick. Amen.

Living it out

There is forgiveness with [the Lord]. « Psalm 130:4

Chances are you need to forgive someone for something they have said or done to you, or you need to ask forgiveness from someone whom you have wronged. Choose one of the options below and begin to rectify the situation.

Option One
FORGIVE SOMEONE

Spend a few minutes thinking about a person you are having trouble forgiving and ask yourself the following questions:

1. Who is the person and what was the situation that hurt you?
2. What, if anything, have you done about it?
3. What are some ways that would help you get past those feelings of hurt and the grudge you hold against the person? (Perhaps ask God for the grace to forgive the person, talk to or write a note to the person, ask a trusted person to mediate the situation, or add your own suggestions.)

Now make the commitment to do something about this situation.

I need to forgive (name)_____. I will begin that process with God's help by

_____

_____

_____

_____

_____

_____

_____

_____

_____

_____

Option Two
ASK FOR FORGIVENESS

Spend a few minutes thinking about someone from whom you need to seek forgiveness and ask yourself the following questions:

1. What was the situation in which you hurt that person?
2. What, if anything, have you done about it?
3. What are some ways that you could start the process of asking for forgiveness?

Now make the commitment to do something about this situation.

I need to ask (name)_____ to forgive me. I will begin that process with God's help by

_____

_____

_____

_____

_____

_____

_____

_____

_____

_____

Results: What are the results of your act of forgiveness or forgiving?

_____

_____

_____

_____

_____

_____

_____

_____

NOTES

1. 2 Samuel 11
2. Genesis 18:1-15
3. Exodus 2:11-15
4. Judges 16
5. Jonah 1
6. Acts 8:1-3; 9:1-31
7. Matthew 18:21-35
8. Corrie ten Boom, *The Hiding Place* (Tappan, New Jersey: Fleming H. Revell, 1971), 215.

009
GOSSIP

I will speak noble things, and from my lips will come what
is right; for my mouth will utter truth. « Proverbs 8:6-7

Tame your tongue

Keep your tongue from evil, and your lips from speaking deceit. « Psalm 34:13

How do you define gossip? This is my definition: The spreading of hurtful remarks about others and something mighty hard to not participate in even when you know it is wrong.

Why do people gossip? Probably for many different reasons, among them:

1. They like appearing to be "in the know."
2. They build themselves up by putting someone else down.
3. They like entertaining their friends and being the center of attention.
4. They may be paying back someone whom they do not like or who has hurt them.

The primary reason people gossip can be summarized by one phrase: self-importance. Who doesn't want to be important and "in the know"?

Who doesn't want to be important and "in the know"?

The tongue can do either great good or great harm. The author of the book of James knew this and wrote: "The tongue is a small member, yet it boasts of great exploits. How great a forest is set ablaze by a small fire! And the tongue is a fire."[1] We have our work cut out for us to tame the exploits of a careless tongue and to put out the fires that uncurbed speech can create.

prayer » God, even though it is really tempting to participate in gossip, give me the desire to use my mouth for building up rather than tearing down. I think I'll need the power of the Holy Spirit to make this happen. Amen.

94

Stick to the truth

Whoever utters slander is a fool. « Proverbs 10:18

You've probably played the game of telephone where everyone sits in a circle and someone whispers a sentence to his or her neighbor. That person then whispers the same sentence to the next person, and so it continues until the sentence has been whispered all around the circle. Rarely is the final sentence at all similar to the original one.

Recently I played the game with a group of teens and whispered the sentence: "Greg bought a rubber chicken and will now do some magic with it." When the telephone game concluded, the last person in the circle announced the sentence as "Craig ate some rubber chickens and is now a magnet on the fridge." If only all the whispers we hear as truth would be so innocent.

Consider being the one who stops the gossip

Keisha did not pass her driver's test the first time she went to get her license. During homeroom she shared this disappointing and embarrassing news with a friend, and at the end of the school day someone Keisha barely knew passed by her in the hall and said, "Wow! I've never known anyone to fail the driver's test five times. That must be some kind of record!" One of the hazards of gossip is that often the truth gets altered beyond recognition, just like in the game of telephone, often with painful consequences.

Spreading information, even if we think it is coming from a reliable source, can be risky. It might be entirely untrue and, worse yet, hurtful and untrue. Consider being the one who stops the gossip. A little test before you pass on gossip might be to ask yourself, Would I be hurt if this piece of information was being spread about me? If the answer is yes, be brave—squash it!

prayer » **God, if I am tempted today to share something unkind about someone, help me be brave and stop the gossip—just as I would want someone to do for me. Amen.**

It pays to squash gossip

All the words of my mouth are righteous; there is nothing twisted or crooked in them. « Proverbs 8:8

Let's face it. Talking unkindly about others is standard fare almost anywhere we go—even at church, I am sorry to say. Molly, a recent newcomer to church, was in a bathroom stall in the church basement when girls from the youth group came into the restroom. She overheard one of them excitedly pass on some news—something totally untrue and extremely unkind—all about Molly. The second youth responded, "Wait until the youth group hears this!" Molly was devastated to think that the girls believed such nonsense and were eager to pass the untruths on to others. She waited until the girls were gone before she left the bathroom; then she walked out of the church and never returned.

Talking unkindly about others is standard fare almost anywhere we go

It is unfortunate that the girls gossiped in the first place, but the story still might have had a different ending if the second teen would have made a conscious effort to stop her friend from passing on unsubstantiated and unkind rumors. Making an effort to refrain from gossip takes a lot of courage and might make you a bit uncomfortable or unpopular with your peers. But refraining from gossip pays great dividends in three ways: you will certainly please God; you will save someone embarrassment and hurt; you will be a better, happier, and more contented person, someone with a clear conscience who can declare, as in the Proverb above, that "there is nothing twisted or crooked in [the words of my mouth]."

A boy in the youth group where I attend church has been described as someone who never says anything unkind about anyone or anything. I cannot think of a more noble and enviable way to be identified.

prayer » The author of the Psalms wrote, "Let the words of my mouth...be acceptable to you, O Lord."[2] I pray that my words can be acceptable to you, God. Amen.

Let's get practical

To watch over mouth and tongue is to keep out of trouble.
« Proverbs 21:23

Gossip sneaks up on you. It might begin as ordinary conversation about someone, something that seems informational, innocent, and mundane. But when the conversation becomes mean-spirited or sensationalistic or petty or exaggerated or hurtful or downright untrue, gossip has reared its ugly head.

Gossip is the opposite of what Christians are asked to do

Gossip is the opposite of what Christians are asked to do: "love your neighbor as yourself."[3] The Apostle Paul writes more about this kind of love:

> If I speak in the tongues of mortals and of angels, but do not have love, I am a noisy gong or a clanging cymbal . . . . Love is kind; love is not envious or boastful or arrogant or rude . . . It does not rejoice in wrongdoing, but rejoices in the truth.[4]

How can you avoid becoming a "noisy gong or "clanging cymbal"? Here are a few practical ways to deal with gossip:

1. Pray that you'll have the courage to stop gossip.
2. Find something kind to say about the person who is being gossiped about.
3. Ask, "Are you sure about that?" Or suggest, "We really should check out the facts before spreading that around."
4. Walk away from the situation.
5. Refuse to pass along information that is not anyone else's business or that is hurtful or unproven.
6. Apologize to the person who has been hurt by gossip.
7. Be courageous and discuss with your friends the potential hurt that gossip causes.

prayer » I don't want to participate in gossip, God, but I still find myself doing it more than I want to. Even though some of my friends might think I'm weird, help me find good ways to stop this habit. Help me find ways to build up others rather than tear them down. Help me love my neighbors as I love myself. I pray these things in Jesus' name. Amen.

Keep gossip from being a habit

The mouths of fools pour out folly . . . [but] a gentle tongue is a tree of life. « Proverbs 15:2, 4

Gossip can become a habit, a behavior that is repeated over and over until it becomes second nature, something ingrained to the point that it is done without much thought. Have you ever thought about gossip as a habit?

Habits are hard to break. When I was little, I sucked my thumb so much my parents tried everything they could think of to break me of the habit. What eventually worked was their insistence that I wear a sock on my left hand whenever I was at home—even to eat, even to sleep. (To this day I can visualize that big red and white athletic sock on my hand.)

I did not plan on becoming a six-year-old thumb sucker. But gradually it just happened, and soon it became something I did without even thinking about it, something I could not stop doing without conscious hard work and careful attention. Likewise, I think we get swept up into the habit of gossiping without setting out to become insensitive or mean. It is too bad that we can't put a big white athletic sock over our mouths when they get out of control.

> *I did not plan on becoming a six-year-old thumb sucker*

But, thank God, we have something better than a sock. We have the assurance that with God's help habits can be broken. The Bible says, "Ask, and it will be given you."[5] Breaking the habit of gossip may not happen overnight, and it may not be easy, but with God's guidance and your willingness to cultivate self-awareness and courage, you'll be a better person for your hard work.

prayer » Keep me from gossiping, God. It is so easy to get caught up in the habit and so hard to stop. Give me strength over and over again to do the right thing. Thank you. Amen.

Tune your heart, fix your mouth

Out of the abundance of the heart the mouth speaks.
« Matthew 12:34

In Matthew 12 Jesus says that a good tree will bear good fruit, but a bad tree will bear bad fruit. Likewise, a good person will bring forth good things, and an evil person will bring forth evil things. Jesus takes this warning one step further and tells the religious establishment that they will have to give an account for every careless and unkind word that they have ever uttered.[6] Will we, too, have to give an account for every careless and unkind word that we have ever uttered?

Out of our mouths comes what is in our hearts

Jesus wants us to understand that out of our mouths comes what is in our hearts. If we are filled with jealousy, pettiness, meanness, arrogance, and narrow-mindedness, the fruit of our speech will be those same things. But if we are filled with love, kindness, compassion, empathy, and peace, our speech will reflect those things.

Honestly consider these questions about gossip:
1. Is my speech filled more with compliments, encouragement, and sympathy or with gossip?
2. When someone is being gossiped about, do I look for opportunities to say something nice about that person, change the subject, or, at the very least, say nothing at all?
3. How quickly do I rush to pass on the latest gossip?

prayer » God, I pray that what comes from my mouth is kind and not mean-spirited; encouraging and not petty; grace-filled and not arrogant; truthful and not exaggerated. In the name of Jesus, Amen.

Living it out

Rash words are like sword thrusts, but the tongue of the wise brings healing. « Proverbs 12:18

As the Scripture indicates, wise speech brings healing instead of injury. Consider being a "healer" with your mouth, either by using it wisely or keeping it shut.

Observation

Be attentive to the gossip you hear this week. Choose one incident of gossip and record your answers to these questions: Who was the gossip about? Who shared it with you? Where were you when you heard the gossip? Were you the only one who heard it? Did you pass the gossip along? Why or why not?

_____

_____

_____

_____

_____

_____

_____

_____

_____

_____

_____

_____

_____

_____

Challenge

In the next week, make the commitment at least one time not to participate in gossip.

Reflect on the Challenge

After your mini-moratorium on gossip, record some of your findings and feelings. How difficult was it to refrain from gossip? Did others notice your non-participation? If so, what was their reaction? Did you feel better or worse for refraining from gossip? Were you able to offer kind words instead of gossip? Are you willing to make a concerted effort to be a non-gossiper? What plans would you make for that to happen?

_____

_____

_____

_____

_____

_____

_____

_____

_____

_____

_____

_____

_____

_____

NOTES

1. James 3:5-6
2. Psalm 19:14
3. Mark 12:31a
4. 1 Corinthians 13:1, 4-6
5. Matthew 7:7
6. Matthew 12:33-37

010

FAITHFUL ATTRACTIONS— YOUR SEXUAL SELF

God created humankind in his image, in the image of God he created them; male and female he created them. « Genesis 1:27

Complete as you are

It was you who formed my inward parts; you knit me together in my mother's womb. I praise you, for I am fearfully and wonderfully made. « Psalm 139:13-14

One thing I hope you never lose sight of is how awesome you are—just as you are right now, right this minute. God "knit you together" the way you were intended to be; God's special creation made in the actual image of God.

> *You do not need a date on Saturday night to make you a worthwhile person*

So what does this have to do with dating and sex? All too often in our culture self-worth is tied to our success with dating or being in a sexual relationship. I know a young woman who is obsessed with having a boyfriend. She tells me she feels unpopular and incomplete if she is not dating anyone. When one relationship ends, she hurries to become involved in another, often choosing a person based on availability rather than on attraction or compatibility.

If you are in a healthy and compatible dating relationship, that is great. But if not, keep in mind that such a relationship is not the barometer for your personal happiness. You do not need a date on Saturday night to make you a worthwhile person. You are special, important, and whole with or without a boyfriend or girlfriend.

prayer » God, I am somebody special because you created me. I need no other person in my life to complete me. I am whole and wonderful just the way I am. Thank you for this creation—me! In Jesus' name, Amen.

Whom will you date?

If you find [wisdom], you will find a future. « Proverbs 24:14

Mike reluctantly went to the party at Leigh's house. He would have preferred to stay home and watch the ballgame, but Leigh was one of his best friends, and he knew she would be disappointed if he didn't show up. He was so glad he did. Ten minutes after arriving, he spotted a girl he had never met: Leigh's cousin, Krista, as it turned out. With sweaty palms and a stammering voice, he approached her and introduced himself. For the next three hours they talked comfortably, and that evening was the beginning of a long and close relationship.

What attracted Mike and Krista to each other? What physical characteristics do you look for in a person you could become interested in knowing better? What personality characteristics do you hope to find in a person you would like to date? How important is it to seek out someone whom your parents would approve of? Does it matter to you that the person you are attracted to is a Christian?

It is prudent to be wise, alert, careful, deliberate, and downright picky in choosing whom to date

It takes wisdom and discernment to choose someone with whom to have a successful relationship. It is a bonus if the person is physically attractive, but you likely know that what matters more is that the person treats you well, is kind and considerate, is not controlling or abusive, and is a person of faith. My mother used to say to me, "Only date someone you can see yourself marrying." That irritated me every time she said it. "It's just a date," I would say. "I have no plans to marry the guy! I'm just in high school." But guess what? I did end up marrying one of those high school guys. You may not have a similar experience, but it is prudent to be wise, alert, careful, deliberate, and downright picky in choosing whom to date.

prayer » **God, help me use wisdom and good sense when I think about the person with whom I would like to have a relationship. In Jesus' name, Amen.**

The Bible is pro-sex

Let him kiss me with the kisses of his mouth! How beautiful you are, my love, how very beautiful.
« Song of Solomon 1:2; 4:1

Whatever is true, whatever is honorable, whatever is just, whatever is pure, whatever is pleasing, whatever is commendable, if there is any excellence and if there is anything worthy of praise, think about these things.
« Philippians 4:8

The Bible gets the anti-sex stigma because it endorses the pleasurable and procreative nature of sex as belonging *within* marriage. As you know, there are many alternative values in our society: most people see sex as acceptable before marriage; many even see sex as okay with people other than your spouse; sex can be with multiple partners; sex can be for sale; sex may include commitment, but not necessarily. You cannot open a magazine, flip through television channels, or listen to the radio without being exposed to the normalcy of sex before marriage or the high rate of marital infidelity. Pornography is no further away than a few clicks on a laptop. Sex shops and strip clubs abound. Sex is big business!

God created humans to love each other and called that creation "good"

Contrary to what many people think, the Bible is not anti-sex. God created humans to love each other and called that creation "good."[1] If you have never read the little book Song of Solomon (also called Song of Songs), tucked between Ecclesiastes and Isaiah in the Old Testament, check it out. I dare say you'll be surprised. In the Bible, sex is sanctioned and welcomed and celebrated and honored. In addition to procreation, God intends sexual intimacy to bring pleasure, satisfaction, beauty, comfort, and oneness.

Philippians 4:8-9 offers a good anchor for our attitudes toward sexuality. The writer encourages us to think about the things that are true and honorable and pure and beautiful and respected. Those are the kind of thoughts that will anchor us to healthy morality.

prayer » In all things make me true, honorable, right, pure, beautiful, and respected. In the holy name of Jesus, Amen.

Physical reasons not to have sex yet

Don't you know that your body is the temple of the Holy Spirit who lives in you and was given to you by God?
« 1 Corinthians 6:19 (*NLT*)

A youth wishing to remain abstinent must feel a little like a salmon swimming upstream against the strong pull of active hormones and the prevailing cultural notions about sex. Movies and the media tell us that casual or premarital sex is normal; if it feels good, it must be right; and if everyone is doing it, why not me?

Movies and the media tell us that casual or premarital sex is normal

Studies indicate that seven out of ten youth have had sexual intercourse by the age of nineteen.[2] Add the number of youth who participate in oral and/or anal sex, and the percentages skyrocket; those sexual acts are just as intimate physically, mentally, and spiritually.

Even those who have no qualms about youth sex can't deny that giving in to the powerful lure of sex involves physical risks and consequences:

- Teenage pregnancy. Approximately 750,000 teenage girls become pregnant each year in the United Sates. That means that approximately 1.5 million girls *and* boys are affected by teenage pregnancy every year.[3]
- Sexually transmitted diseases (STDs) or sexually transmitted infections (STIs). There are over fifty possible STDs and STIs that can be contracted by unprotected sex,[4] and many of these do not manifest themselves until later years, perhaps having been passed on to countless unsuspecting partners.

Even with "safe" sex practices there is no guarantee that either pregnancy or STDs will be avoided, and both are potentially life-changing consequences of sex.

prayer » **God, do you know how hard it is to be a teenager? Amen.**

Spiritual and emotional reasons not to have sex yet

There's more to sex than mere skin on skin. Sex is as much spiritual mystery as physical fact. As written in Scripture, "The two become one." Since we want to become spiritually one with the Master, we must not pursue the kind of sex that avoids commitment and intimacy, leaving us more lonely than ever—the kind of sex that can never "become one . . ." In sexual sin we violate the sacredness of our own bodies, these bodies that were made for God-given and God-modeled love, for "becoming one" with another.
« 1 Corinthians 6:16-18 (*The Message*)

Your body is sacred

As serious as the physical dangers of teenage sex are, perhaps the more significant reasons to abstain are emotional and spiritual.

- Just because you are physically able to have sex, it doesn't mean that you are emotionally mature enough for sex—even if you love your boyfriend or girlfriend.
- You may find sex without a significant relationship momentarily satisfying, but it will not lead to the commitment and intimacy God intended.
- Your body is God's temple and the place where God chooses to reside.[5] Your body is sacred and made for God-given and God-modeled love. Reread the Scripture above.
- When you share your body with another person in the most intimate way, it is a gift of great significance; but it is a gift best unwrapped and fully explored in the context of the committed relationship of marriage.
- Damaged reputations from promiscuity are difficult to repair.
- Guard the gift of your sexuality carefully. It is *yours* to give and never for anyone to take against your will.
- Even if you have already been sexually active, it is possible to abstain in the future, until you are married (sometimes called secondary virginity).

prayer » There is much to ponder, God. Give me the desire to do your will in all things, including in sexual matters. Amen.

Stand up to temptation

Stay away from lusts which tempt young people. Pursue what has God's approval. « 2 Timothy 2:22 (*GWT*)

There is a saying: "If alcohol is a problem for you, don't live across the street from a bar." This can translate to sexual matters, too.

- If online pornography is a problem for you, put parental blocks on your own computer and move it to the most public place in your house.
- If you are invited to a party where you know there will be sexual games and casual experimentation, don't go.
- If you receive an explicit "sext" message, delete it immediately and refuse to send the pictures any farther.
- If sexual intimacy is difficult to resist with your boyfriend or girlfriend, double date or go on group dates.

Be open about your decision to not have sex before marriage. The more people who know of your decision, the harder it will be to be to break your word. Find a group of trustworthy friends or adults that you can talk to about your temptations. Believe it or not, almost every adult you know struggled with the same things you are going through. Learn from their advice, wisdom, and experience. Push your youth leader, Sunday school teacher, or pastor to be open and accessible to teens about the frustrations and struggles with all aspects of sexuality.

It takes boldness, self-awareness, self-assurance, courage, and maturity to stay on a moral course. But with God's help, you can be strong! Helping us resist temptation is one of God's specialties. Tell God your most secret of secrets; there is not a thing that you do, say, or think that will surprise God. And when necessary, confess your wrongdoing and accept God's forgiveness. Partner with God to keep your life holy and whole.

Partner with God to keep your life holy

prayer » **God, give me strength and courage. Be with me. Love me. Forgive me. Be proud of me. In Jesus' name, Amen.**

Living it out

Some of you say, "We can do anything we want to." But I tell you that not everything is good for us.
« 1 Corinthians 6:12 (*CEV*)

It was Sunday evening, and I was driving home after speaking about the Twelve Steps of Intimacy to a youth group in a nearby town. The group was small that evening, just five teens, and I felt that I had done a poor job of connecting with them. They seemed embarrassed about what I was presenting and kept their eyes averted most of the evening. The discussion was negligible, and the little that happened was a dialogue between the youth leader and myself. All the way home I second-guessed myself about what I could have said or done differently to better engage the youth. By the time I reached home I had pretty much talked myself into thinking it was a wasted evening for all concerned.

But God does amazing things, and two weeks later I got a phone call from my youth leader friend telling me that one of the guys who was present that evening had just left her office. He had come by to tell her that he was able to use the steps of intimacy as a discussion starter for a conversation he needed to have with his girlfriend.

"But that isn't all," she said. "What you presented was a good discussion starter for Sunday school the next week. Those who did not attend the youth group meeting quizzed the others about the Twelve Step chart, and the general consensus was how helpful it was to talk and think about this while 'not in the heat of the moment.'"

The Twelve Steps of Intimacy concept was introduced by anthropologist Desmond Morris. His theory was that a couple needed to progress through twelve steps slowly and deliberately in order to create a long-lasting and satis-fying sexual relationship. Although Morris was applying his concept to adults, I was introduced to the Twelve Steps at a youth conference where it was suggested that youth could use the chart to help plan where in the twelve steps they would voluntarily and deliberately stop their sexual activity.

TWELVE STEPS OF INTIMACY[6]

1. Eye to Body
2. Eye to Eye
3. Voice to Voice
4. Hand to Hand
5. Hand to Shoulder
6. Hand to Waist
7. Mouth to Mouth
8. Hand to Head
9. Hand to Body
10. Mouth to Body
11. Touching Below the Waist
12. Sexual Intercourse

Steps one through six are obviously less intimate than steps seven through twelve. Deciding where on the list you are not willing to go beyond is an important and mature thing to do. I'm guessing most Christian youth want someone to tell them where on the chart they should stop their sexual activity. Although I have an opinion about where on the list of steps teens should stop, this is your discernment to make. Reflect on the following questions when discerning:

- Where along the spectrum of sexual activities listed on the chart do you think you should stop and go no further?
- Do you think it a good idea to talk about this chart with the person you are dating?
- If you are hesitant to bring up this discussion with that person, why is that?
- If you and your significant other disagree about where on the chart the sexual activity should stop, how will you reach agreement?
- What will you do if your boyfriend or girlfriend insists upon greater sexual intimacy than you are comfortable with?

Thinking about these things before passion drives your actions will help you avoid a level of sexual intimacy you will later regret.

God celebrates and cares about your sexuality. Include God in your dating relationships and discernment about morality. Pray about your sexuality.

- Thank God for creating you as a sexual being.
- If you would like to be in a significant dating relationship but are not, pray about it.
- If you are currently in a relationship, ask God for guidance to know what is appropriate sexual behavior for you and the person you are dating.
- If you are in a relationship and have crossed beyond the boundaries of sexual behavior that you are comfortable with, pray for the courage to discuss this with your boyfriend or girlfriend.
- If you regret having traveled further along the steps of intimacy than you think appropriate, ask God for forgiveness and for the strength to refrain from doing so in the future.
- If you are in an abusive dating relationship, pray for the strength to leave that situation immediately.
- If you feel like you need to discuss any aspect of sexuality, ask God for guidance on whom you might approach with your questions and concerns.

NOTES

1. Genesis 1:26-31
2. J. C. Abma et al. *Vital and Health Statistics*, Series 23, No. 30, 2010, http://www .guttmacher.org/pubs/ FB-ATSRH.html
3. K. Kost et al. *U.S. Teenage Pregnancies, Births and Abortions: National and State Trends and Trends by Race and Ethnicity*, 2010, http://www.guttmacher.org/ pubs/USTPtrends.pdf
4. Center for Disease Control and Prevention, Atlanta, U.S. Department of Health and Human Services, 2009, http://www.cdc.gov/std /stats08/trends.htm
5. 1 Corinthians 6:19
6. The Kansas Department of Health and Environment, Kansas Abstinence Education Program, 2008–2011, http://www.gonnawait.org /teens/love_12_steps.html

011
MY MONEY, GOD'S MONEY

The lover of money will not be satisfied with money;
nor the lover of wealth, with gain. « Ecclesiastes 5:10

Generosity beyond imagination

[God speaking] Will anyone rob God? Yet you are robbing me! "How are we robbing you?" In your tithes and offerings." « Malachi 3:8

After reading today's Scripture, you might be saying, "Stop right there! I'm just a teenager. In what ways can I possibly be robbing God? Aren't tithes (10 percent of one's income) and offerings something my parents need to worry about, something the adults at church need to take responsibility for? Besides, even with my allowance and all the birthday money my grandparents gave me, I still don't have enough money to make any difference in this world. The needs are too great, and I'm just one person."

I grew up in a house where parents insisted the children's money be divided by this formula: one-third went to the church or to a charity of our choice; one-third went into a savings account; and one-third was available for personal spending. This applied to money we earned, money we found, and money we were given as gifts.

> ## The needs are too great, and I'm just one person

Kind of extreme, wasn't it? As a teenager I thought this distribution extremely weak in the personal spending category, but I did learn some valuable lessons about money from this formula. First, I learned that my money counted in kingdom work, regardless of how little I actually contributed. Second, I learned about my family's philosophy of money, and the message was loud and clear: saving money is important and giving to the church is non-negotiable. Have you ever talked to your family about money? What are your family's priorities when it comes to money? How would you describe your family's philosophy of money?

prayer » **Even though I'm a teenager, God, I recognize that my money is also your money. Amen.**

114

The love of money

For the love of money is a root of all kinds of evil, and in their eagerness to be rich some have wandered away from the faith and pierced themselves with many pains.
« 1 Timothy 6:10

Some people think the Bible says "money is the root of all evil." But in Paul's letter to his young friend, Timothy, he says, "The *love* of money is a root of all kinds of evil" (emphasis mine). Unarguably, money is absolutely necessary in our world: it puts food on our tables, clothes on our backs, and roofs over our heads. But an obsession with acquiring, hoarding, or spending money can cause problems. Paul says that an "eagerness to be rich"[1] can lead us to ignore the obvious needs around us. Jesus bluntly says you cannot serve both God and wealth at the same time.[2]

Scrooge's love of money resulted in great loneliness.

In the book *A Christmas Carol,* Ebenezer Scrooge, a miserly old man, spends Christmas Eve counting his stash of gold coins. His love of money has resulted in substantial wealth, but also great loneliness. During the night, the angels of Christmas past, present, and future visit Scrooge and show him through wild and vivid dreams how much he has hurt others and himself in the drive for more and more wealth.[3] Scrooge has fallen into the trap that today's Scripture warns us about: In our eagerness to be rich, we wander away from faith and pierce ourselves with pain. Fortunately, by the end of the tale, Scrooge releases his greed and adopts a new spirit of generosity.

It is easy to see how "off the mark" Scrooge was in his love of money. It isn't always so easy to see how much the love of money has affected our own lives.

prayer » I want to keep from having an unhealthy love of money, God. I want to set my priorities for the future based on more than how rich I'll be someday. In the name of Jesus, Amen.

The pleasure of a little giving

For where your treasure is, there your heart will be also.
« Matthew 6:21

In the Gospel of Luke, Jesus tells his disciples to be aware of the ultra-religious folks who strut around hoping people notice how important and wealthy they are. To illustrate his point, he takes the disciples to the temple to observe the worshippers putting money into the offering boxes. Before long, several of those religious people whom Jesus had just warned the disciples about enter the temple and pompously drop their money into the offering boxes. They make a big production of how much they are giving and sigh contentedly with an air of "look how holy I am!" They look around to see if anyone is casting admiring glances their way.

Never assume that the amount you are able to give back to God is insignificant

Along comes a poor widow who drops two small and insignificant copper coins into an offering box. Jesus is instantly moved and tells the disciples to look at what just happened. This woman has given an offering far more impressive than all of those rich people combined. They gave out of their abundance and, because they had so much, wouldn't even miss what they parted with. But she, who is poorer than the rich could ever imagine, has given *everything* she has to live on.[4]

As a young person, likely without many financial resources, you should never assume that the amount you are able to give back to God is insignificant. Your giving, especially when accompanied by cheerfulness, honors and pleases God.

prayer » Generous God, put in my heart the desire to give to your work in the world. I know you honor all gifts that are given with joy and gratitude. In Jesus' name, Amen.

116

Generosity—whether or not you feel generous

Then the people rejoiced because these had given willingly.
« 1 Chronicles 29:9

My grandmother used to say, "Happiness leads to generosity and generosity leads to happiness." This is the classic chicken and egg debate. Which comes first? Generosity or happiness? (She also used to say "It is better to give than receive,"[5] but probably everyone's grandmother said that.)

When I am happy and things are going well, I automatically feel more generous—generous with my money, my time, and my words. Conversely, when I am generous I automatically feel happier. When I am feeling sad and unhappy, it is difficult to feel generous, but, believe it or not, that is the perfect time to do something for someone else. Generosity is not a normal or natural outcome of being sad, so I might have to make myself be generous when I am "down in the dumps." What I have noticed, even though the generosity may be a bit contrived, is that it is pretty difficult to remain unhappy when focusing on others rather than myself.

Which comes first? Generosity or happiness?

Here's my challenge for when you are feeling sad: buy a friend some ice cream, offer to do the dishes or wash the family car without being asked, buy new crayons or markers for a Sunday school class at church, write a note of appreciation to a favorite teacher, anonymously slip a few bills into the locker slots of someone at school who you know is struggling financially.

A word of warning: generosity will not only make you happy, it can be addicting.

prayer » **Help me, generous God, to find ways to be generous with my money, with my time, and with my words. In the name of Jesus, Amen.**

Contentment—a key to happiness

Keep your lives free from the love of money, and be content with what you have. « Hebrews 13:5

I find that being content with what I have is a little harder than it sounds because there always seems to be just one more thing I want. I wish there was some magic formula I could follow or some button I could push to keep from slipping into the "gotta have it" mindset.

When we never seem satisfied . . . it might be time to examine our wants versus our needs

Being content certainly runs counter to what advertisers and media try to sell us. Something bigger, better, faster, and more attractive—that's what we need! The newest styles of jeans, phones, computers, cars, gaming systems, you name it.

It is not that all the things we want are bad things, but when we never seem satisfied with our acquisitions and are overly focused on the next thing we must have, it might be time to examine our *wants* versus our *needs*. Consider asking these questions the next time you are about to buy something. Is buying this absolutely necessary? Can I wait for two days to make the purchase in order to gauge how much I really want or need it? Is my level of contentment and satisfaction really based on my ability to buy this? Is there anything else I could do with this money that would help someone and, at the same time, give me a feeling of satisfaction and joy?

prayer » **God, help me be more content with what I have. Help me grasp less at things that only give me fleeting happiness. In the name of Jesus, who has quite a lot to say about money, Amen.**

118

Camels, needles, and wealth

It is easier for a camel to go through the eye of a needle than for someone who is rich to enter the kingdom of God. « Luke 18:25

All day long Jesus speaks to large crowds of people, and by sundown his disciples are hungry and grumpy. Despite Jesus' protests, they hurry the crowds away and finally sit down to enjoy their simple dinner. A young man who has lingered all day at the edge of the crowd moves to the center of the little gathering. It is obvious from the exquisitely fine clothes the man wears that he is quite wealthy.

"Jesus," he begins, "you have given me much to think about today, and I want to know what I can do to ensure this eternal life you spoke about." Jesus answers as he tears off a bite of bread and shares it with the young man: "Keep the commandments: do not commit marital infidelity, do not murder, do not steal or lie, and always honor your parents."

"I do all those things," the man replies. Jesus pauses a moment, takes of sip of water, and looks intently into the man's eyes. "Then," he continues, "give half of everything you own to the poor." The man furrows his brow and remains silent for a long while. Without a word, he turns and walks away. With deep sadness Jesus says to his disciples, "It is easier for a camel to go through the eye of a needle than for a rich person to enter heaven."[6]

Give until it brings joy

I don't think Jesus is saying that the only way we can be part of the kingdom of God is to literally give away half of all we own (let alone everything we own as he says elsewhere in the Gospel of Luke[7]). Instead, I think he is saying that heaven-bound people must care for the poor by giving sacrificially. Each of us will receive our own Holy Spirit challenge as to what sacrificial giving might be for our circumstances. One way I have heard this explained is that we should "give until it hurts." I would reframe that by saying we should "give until it brings joy."

prayer » Let my giving bring joy to others and a smile to my heart. Amen.

Living it out

Do not store up for yourselves treasures on earth, where moth and rust consume and where thieves break in and steal, but store up for yourselves treasures in heaven, where neither moth nor rust consumes and where thieves do not break in and steal. « Matthew 6:19-20

Choose Option One or Option Two—or do both!

Option One

Below you will find several examples of sacrificial generosity. Choose one, or create your own activity, and record your results upon completion.

1. Go on a "loose change scavenger hunt" looking for coins in couch cushions, in the bottom of purses, in the console of the car, etc. Consider asking everyone in your household to join in the fun. Take the money and place it in the offering plate at church or give to a favorite charity.

2. Choose three pieces of *stylish* clothes that are currently in your closet and donate them to a local charitable organization without shopping for replacements.

3. Every time you spend money on yourself this coming week, even if just buying a candy bar, set aside one dollar. When you accumulate enough, purchase grocery store gift cards with this money and give them either to your pastor or principal to distribute as needs come to their attention.

RESULTS

Record what activity you did and briefly describe the experience. Any reflections or observations?

_____

_____

_____

_____

_____

_____

_____

_____

_____

_____

_____

Option Two

Interview a parent(s) regarding his or her ideas about money. You might start with the following questions: Does our family routinely give money to church or charities? How does our family decide how much money to give to church or charities? Do we write an offering or charity check before we pay other bills, or do we give church or charities an amount that is left after we pay the bills? How does our family go about deciding how to spend discretionary money? Does our family's money belong to us or to God?

RESULTS

Jot down the important points of the discussion you have with your parent(s).

_____

_____

_____

_____

_____

_____

_____

_____

_____

_____

_____

_____

_____

NOTES

1. 1 Timothy 6:10
2. Matthew 6:24 and Luke 16:13
3. Charles Dickens, *A Christmas Carol* (London: Chapman and Hall, 1843).
4. Luke 20:45–21:4
5. Acts 20:35
6. Luke 18:18-25
7. Luke 12:33

012
THE WORDS WE USE

Let the words of my mouth and the meditation of my heart be acceptable to you, O LORD, my rock and my redeemer. « Psalm 19:14

The mighty mouth

Let no one despise your youth, but set the believers an example in speech and conduct, in love, in faith, in purity. « 1 Timothy 4:12

Our speech—what a mighty tool for good and a powerful one for hurt! Words that come from our mouths can build up or tear down, praise or demean. Carefully uttered words can heal, encourage, and fortify. Unthinking words can injure, offend, and destroy.

Paul tells his friend Timothy that even though he is young, he can still set an example in his speech and conduct, approaching both with love, faith, and purity.

The words we use are completely in our control

Why is good speech important? Because others are watching you, for one reason. Whether you like it or not, your speech and conduct say something about you as a person of faith. If your peers know you are a follower of Jesus, they are going to be listening to what comes out of your mouth and watching how you live your life.

The words we use are completely in our control. We choose whether to lie, backstab, gossip, exaggerate, or swear. We choose whether to tell the truth, compliment, or encourage.

The writer of the book of James says, "From the same mouth come blessing and cursing, . . .this ought not to be so."[1] An Old Testament proverb reminds us: "To watch over mouth and tongue is to keep out of trouble."[2]

prayer » God, may the words I say today be ones that both you and I are proud of. Help me examine the way I talk in honest and careful ways so that people see you through me. In the name of Jesus, Amen.

Honor God with speech

You shall not make wrongful use of the name of the LORD your God, for the LORD will not acquit anyone who misuses his name. « Exodus 20:7

Every tongue shall give praise to God. « Romans 14:11

Recently I was watching a movie but had to finally turn it off because I could no longer tolerate the constant use of one or more misguided variations on the name of God. It was a fairly engaging story, but the blatant misuse of God's name hammered away at my sensibilities.

"What's the big deal?" my children used to say when I objected to this kind of language in a movie we watched together. "We hear it all the time and hardly notice it. We don't use that kind of language just because we hear it every-where, Mom." That was true—they didn't use that kind of language. But I think that sometimes we hear God's name used inappropriately so often that we become de-sensitized to it.

God tells Moses to write down ten rules for good living.[3] In that list of rules are the commands to honor the Sabbath and one's parents and to not murder, steal, commit adultery, lie, worship any other gods or idols, or be envious of what your neighbor has. And right up alonside of murdering, lying, and stealing is the commandment: Do not make wrongful use of the name of the Lord, your God.

How can we who love God degrade God's name by making it an expletive?

How can we who love God degrade God's name by making it an expletive? As people who love God, it is our privilege to be able to use our speech to praise God.

prayer » I will keep the commandment to revere your name, God. I praise your name, and in the holy name of Jesus, I will try to keep my words respectful. Amen.

Set a guard over the mouth

Their mouths are full of cursing and bitterness.
« Romans 3:14

Set a guard over my mouth, O LORD; keep watch over the door of my lips. « Psalm 141:3

Swearing can show a lack of creativity

It is common for expletives to dot speech in all kinds of places, by all kinds of people, and in all kinds of situations. You may not agree on all of the following points, but I share a few reasons why I personally resist the temptation to use swear words.

- Swearing can show a lack of creativity in speech, especially if used multiple times in the same sentence.
- The avoidance of cursing can be a sign of respect for the people around us, especially for those who are offended and not used to this type of language.
- Swearing can become a habit, and before long we can resort to using it without giving it any thought.
- Because everyone else seems to be swearing isn't a reason to do so myself.
- Dotting my speech with frequent expletives may feel or sound like a cool thing to do as a young person, but how cool would it sound to my boss or small children when I'm forty years old?
- I show signs of self-control when I refrain from bad language.

prayer » "Set a guard over my mouth, O LORD, [and] keep watch over the door of my lips" so that my speech honors you, those around me, and myself. Amen.

Think before speaking

How great a forest is set ablaze by a small fire! And the tongue is a fire. « James 3:5, 6

Have you ever said something that from the moment it was out of your mouth you wished you never would have said it and would have given anything to have another chance to say it differently?

When my daughter was seven, we were scurrying around the house getting ready to host several people for dinner. I was running behind, and she offered to help. Knowing that she was very good at cleaning chores, far beyond most kids her age, I asked her to vacuum the house. She did—the entire house. It took her a long time, and when she was finished, she proudly wanted to show me every room. I was impatient, needing to set the table and finish cooking dinner, but I grudgingly took a few minutes to take the tour of her hard work. When we came to our bedroom there were a few linty fibers on the carpet that she had missed with the sweeper. Out of my mouth came words I still regret twenty-five years later. "I can't believe you missed sweeping this spot. It's in plain sight!" Her little happy face crumbled, her lips quivered, and tears rolled down her cheeks. I still wish I had those seconds back to tell her what a great job she had done and to thank her for being such a helpful little girl. Who really cared about some lint in a room the guests would never even enter? What a shame I did not use my mouth to praise and thank her.

Careless, hasty words can devastate, hurt, maim, and tear down

Careless, hasty words can devastate, hurt, maim, and tear down. Think, think, think before something comes from your mouth. I doubt if you'll ever regret the few extra seconds it takes to think before you speak.

prayer » Help me think before I speak. Help me see how careless words can devastate. Help me keep my mouth shut if my speech is going to hurt someone. In Jesus' name, Amen.

Ambush with smooth talk

Their tongue is a deadly arrow; it speaks deceit through the mouth. They all speak friendly words to their neighbors, but inwardly are planning to lay an ambush.
« Jeremiah 9:8

Erin and Morgan were walking down the hall and passed by Deandra. "Cute skirt, you look great in it!" Erin exclaimed. "No kidding, girl! Wish I had one just like it," added Morgan. "Wow," Deandra thought happily, "they've never complimented me on anything. I think they must like me." Later, in world history class, Deandra's friend told her she had overheard the girls laughing at Deandra's clothes. The friend told Deandra that Morgan had said, "Where do you think she got such an ugly skirt? Even my grandmother wouldn't be caught dead in that!" Deandra felt confused and betrayed.

As today's verse points out, words can seem friendly at the very same time an ambush is about to take place. When someone betrays us with his or her speech, it feels like our heart has been pierced by an arrow. To what purpose did the two girls say they liked the skirt when they clearly did not? Why say anything at all if it isn't true? Why act one way one minute and then another way the next?

No one else is going to monitor your tongue but you

The Apostle Paul reminds us in the book of Colossians: let your speech always be gracious, using words that are kind, courteous, charitable, cordial, polite, and truthful.[4] It is important to pay attention to what comes out of your mouth. No one else is going to monitor your tongue but you. No one else is responsible for what comes out of your mouth but you.

prayer » May my words be gracious. May I think twice before participating in speech that is harmful. May my mouth be full of courteous and truthful words. In the name of Jesus, Amen.

Speak noble words

I will speak noble things, and from my lips will come what is right; for my mouth will utter truth. « Proverbs 8:6-7

Our mouths can, of course, be the instruments for much good.

- Think how good it feels to receive a genuine compliment.
- Think how the comment "good job" can bolster your confidence.
- Think how the phrase "I'm sorry" can heal your pain.
- Think how hearing "I love you" from someone special can make your heart beat faster.
- Think how words of encouragement can give you permission to try new things.
- Think how a phone message from a friend who has moved away can bring a smile to your face.
- Think how a few compassionate words can bring tears to your eyes.
- Think how constructive feedback can lead to positive life changes.

We have the ability to cause great joy with the prudent and kindhearted use of our mouths

We have at our constant disposal the ability to cause great joy with the prudent and kindhearted use of our mouths. It is our privilege to actively seek opportunities to use words of encouragement, truth, and kindness. We owe it to God, to others, and to ourselves to pay attention to our speech, actively looking for ways to use our words in positive and uplifting ways.

prayer » Show me, Lord, where I can use my speech to build up, support, encourage, and praise. Help me be on the lookout for the times I need to say "I'm sorry" or when I can declare "Good job!" May I be lavish with my praise and stingy with my criticism. Hear my prayer, Jesus. Amen.

Living it out

Pleasant words are like a honeycomb, sweetness to the soul and health to the body. « Proverbs 16:24

I once heard about a teacher who was tired of hearing his students poke fun at, ridicule, and badmouth their peers. He gave them an unusual assignment. He passed out new notebooks to each student and asked them to put that day's date on the first page, the next day's date on the second page, and so on until there were seven pages with dates. Next, he had the students put the numbers one to ten under each date.

For the next week, every student was to say something nice to someone at school ten times every day, trying to be sincere and honest with their words. Every time they did that, they were to have the person to whom they spoke sign the page. Their grade would be determined by the number of entries they had. For the first few minutes the class just stared at the teacher as if he might be joking. Eventually one brave soul said, "You're kidding, right?" "Not kidding, class dismissed!" exclaimed the teacher.

One week later, the teacher collected the notebooks to grade. He had noticed a marked lessening of unkind words in his class during the week of the assignment, but he was eager to look at the results. Over eighty percent of the class completed the assignment. And even more surprising, the teacher noticed that by the end of the week, almost all of those who did the homework had added many more numbers to each page.

I never heard whether the experiment had long lasting results. But for a week at least, students were given an opportunity to pay close attention to the possibilities of positive speech.

As a variation of this experiment in kind words, you'll need a box of twenty-five paper clips or twenty-five toothpicks and a plastic sandwich bag that zips open and shut. Each day, for as long as you do this experiment, put a paper clip or toothpick in your sandwich bag every time you say something kind to someone or about someone. Remove a paper clip or toothpick each time you say something unkind to someone or about someone. At the end of each day, tally the number of clips or toothpicks in your bag. Keep track every day of that number. Also subtract that number from twenty-five so you can also keep track of your negative comments per day.

After your experiment is over, reflect on these questions:

1. What was the total number of kind things you said? What was the total number of unkind things you said?

_____

_____

_____

_____

_____

2. Did the results of kind things versus unkind things you said surprise you? Why or why not?

_____

_____

_____

_____

_____

3. Could you tell your actions shifted at all during the experiment?

_____

_____

_____

_____

_____

4. What did you learn about yourself and your speech?

_____

_____

_____

_____

_____

NOTES

1. James 3:10
2. Proverbs 21:23
3. Exodus 20:1-17
4. Colossians 4:6

013
STRESS

My flesh and my heart may fail, but God is the strength
of my heart and my portion forever. « Psalm 73:26

The stress-o-meter

Even youths will faint and be weary, and the young will fall exhausted. « Isaiah 40:30

Some adults just can't fathom how stressed and overwhelmed youth are. They say, "You're young, what could possibly be stressful for you? Just wait until you are grown up then you'll see what real stress is!" As I taught youth Sunday school week after week, I heard firsthand the very real strains and stresses of being a teenager. So I began most Sunday school sessions with a stress-o-meter exercise where each student shared a number from one to ten to indicate the stress level of the past week. The lower the number, the more carefree and stress-free the week had been. A higher number indicated a more stress-filled week. This was a good way for us to keep tabs on each other and to pray for those going through difficult or busy times.

Choose to react to stress in positive ways

All kinds of things can cause you stress: family, friend and dating relationships, acceptance from peers, demands on your time from multiple sources, grades, appearance, extra-curricular activities, getting into college, safety, temptations to use harmful substances, and other things I can't even imagine. You will never escape all stress now or in the future. But here are some helpful things to keep in mind:

1. You can choose to react to stress in positive ways.
2. You can extend a bit of grace to yourself in stressful situations.
3. You can practice saying no to help alleviate some of the stress caused by busyness.
4. You can ask God to be with you.

prayer » God, I know it is normal to be stressed from time to time, but sometimes stress threatens to overtake me. Please be with me and fill me with your presence and calming Spirit. Amen.

Help!

O Lord, make haste to help me! « Psalm 70:1

It's 3:30 and school is out. I quickly head to my locker to grab my gym bag; rush to the locker room and change for the soccer game; play my heart out. We win! My parents are in the stands cheering me on, and once the match is over, Mom hands me a lunch bag so I can eat on the way to my piano lesson.

I sit in the back of the van where the windows are tinted and change back into my clothes. I gulp down the sandwich and carrots, but Mom forgot to bring me a drink. I'm very thirsty after the game, and we pull through a fast-food drive-in to get a large water and another sandwich. I finish eating just as we pull up in front of my piano teacher's house. I grab the music I remembered to put in the car this morning and run into the house. I'm a few minutes late and worried because I had almost no time to practice this week. My teacher, Mrs. Nance, is clearly irritated with me again.

We work hard, but it is clear that we're not going to finish tonight

Dad picks me up and takes me to Rosa's house where my history study group is working on a project we have to present this Friday. The project is half our quarter's grade, and I really need at least a B on it or my GPA is going to drop. We work hard, but it is clear that we're not going to finish tonight. My parents were expecting me home by 9:00, but I call to let them know Rosa's dad will run us all home in another hour or so. I get home at 10:30. Everyone has gone to bed, but there is a note on the counter beside a plate of snickerdoodle cookies. Mom writes, "When are you going to clean the cave we used to call your room?"

I grab a handful of cookies and run upstairs to begin my homework. Wow, I have a lot of homework tonight! I need to study for tomorrow's biology test, analyze a poem for English, and solve three involved math problems for calculus by first hour. And to top it off, I get a text message from my girlfriend asking if I'm ever going to have time for her? I'm tired, overwhelmed, weary, and it's only Tuesday!

prayer » O God—HELP! Amen.

God's promises

Those who wait for the LORD shall renew their strength, they shall mount up with wings like eagles, they shall run and not be weary; they shall walk and not faint.
« Isaiah 40:31

"Hurry up! You're too slow!" Tiana's boss yelled at her in front of the customers. She was working as fast as she could given that the woman at her station could not make up her mind whether to order a fish sandwich or a chicken sandwich. "You're working an hour overtime with no pay to make up for being so slow," her boss demanded fifteen minutes later. "I can't," she timidly replied, "I have play practice." "You work or you're fired, you lazy girl," he threatened. Tiana burst into tears. Her family needed the income from this job, but Ms. McGuire said if she was late for rehearsal one more time, she was out of the production. She didn't know what to do, and she wasn't sure she could handle the stress of work, school, and home any longer.

Over and over we read in the Bible how much we can rely on God's presence

It is no surprise that Tiana was overcome by stress that day. The demands on her time and the unkindness of her boss were overwhelming. Perhaps you've had experiences similar to Tiana's. Over and over we read in the Bible how much we can rely on God's presence in the stressful times of our lives. Here are just two examples of the promises we've been given:

From where will my help come? My help comes from the LORD who made heaven and earth. « Psalm 121:1, 2

Do not fear, for I am with you, do not be afraid, for I am your God; I will strengthen you, I will help you.
« Isaiah 41:10

When you find yourself so stressed and overwhelmed that it is hard to see how you will cope, accept the invitation to rely on the strength, guidance, peace, and rest that God so readily offers. The problems may not go away, but a quick, silent prayer invites God to help you face whatever comes your way.

prayer » God, so many people want so much from me that I'm frazzled. I will try to remember that you give me strength to face whatever comes my way. I'm going to count on your promises and expect that you will help me carry these stresses. In Jesus' name, Amen.

Negative responses to stress

Come to me, all you that are weary and are carrying heavy burdens, and I will give you rest. « Matthew 11:28

Fortunately, most of the stressful times in teenagers' lives are momentary or short lived, and most youth get through them without going to extreme measures. But sometimes the rigors of being a teenager are overwhelming to the point of feeling hopeless, overwhelming to the point of doing harm to oneself. Unbearable stress can lead to serious negative responses: anger, overeating, undereating, bullying, withdrawing from friends and family, drugs, alcohol, sex, stealing, cutting, lying, cheating, smoking, prolonged grouchiness, breaking house rules, skipping school or work, and even suicide.

Dangerous and negative responses to stress can have far-reaching consequences

Dangerous and negative responses to stress can have far-reaching consequences. If you should ever find yourself so distressed that you respond in dangerous ways, it is urgent that you find someone with whom you can share those feelings: your parents, a pastor, a teacher, a relative, a family friend, a trusted peer. You are far too precious to be swallowed up or shattered by overwhelming stress.

In the Scripture above, Jesus invites you to bring your stresses and anxieties, big and little, to him. Sometimes the way the promised rest happens is through the help and guidance of other people. Do not be afraid to ask for help from Jesus and from others.

prayer » Come, Lord Jesus, come. I lay before you all those things that I find stressful in my life. I need you to help carry my burdens. I need you to help me find ways to cope. I need you to send people into my life that I can trust and with whom I can honestly share. Please keep me from harmful and negative behaviors. In your name I pray. Amen.

Positive responses to stress

True to your word, you let me catch my breath and send me in the right direction. « Psalm 23:3 (*The Message*)

May I find hope and humor in whatever comes my way

I asked a group of teens to list positive and healthy ways they respond to the stress in their lives. In no order of importance, this is their list:

- Exercise or take a brisk walk.
- Unload to your grandparents, pastor, parents, sibling, or friend. Never underestimate their support and good advice.
- Drop everything and go out for the biggest chocolate milkshake you can find.
- Talk to your teacher(s) about extra tutoring or for an extension on a project.
- Practice deep breathing exercises.
- Get a good night's sleep even if you don't think you can afford the time.
- Try to spend at least five minutes each day in total quiet.
- Pray.
- Read your Bible.
- Try saying some tongue twisters.
- Before going to sleep each night, write down three good things that happened that day.
- Call or visit a friend who has a calming influence.
- Laugh.
- Practice saying "this is not a life or death matter; this is not a life or death matter; this is not a life or death matter."
- Go to church or youth group even if you have lots of homework.
- Stand on your head.

What positive responses to stress would you add?

prayer » I give you thanks for this day. May I find hope and humor in whatever comes my way. I pray these things in the name of Jesus. Amen.

When worry consumes

Cast all your anxiety on [God] because [God] cares for you.
« 1 Peter 5:7

Gretchen's mother was consumed by worry. She would not allow Gretchen to drive a car because she worried she'd have an accident and become paralyzed. Gretchen could not attend school dances because she might be touched inappropriately while dancing. She couldn't go to sleepovers because she might become sick from lack of sleep. She was not allowed to participate in sports because she might be injured. Gretchen's mother worried about her daughter's weight, grades, ability to get into a prestigious college, and just about every other imaginable thing.

Jesus' disciples were worrywarts, too. He tells them:

> Do not worry about your life or about what you will eat. Do not worry about your body or what you will wear. What good will it do you? Will worrying add a single hour to your life span? Consider the birds of the air and the lilies of the field. They do absolutely nothing to earn their keep, yet God takes care of them. How much more value are you to God than birds and lilies! Do not worry![1]

God takes care of the birds and lilies; God will take care of you

Some worrying is natural and realistic, but some of us (like Gretchen's mother) are inclined to worry excessively. Undue worrying leads to undue stress. If worrying is causing a lot of stress in your life, try pushing the worries right out of your mind by dwelling more on positive thoughts and outcomes than on the negative "what ifs." Move ahead in faith. God takes care of the birds and lilies; God will take care of you.

prayer » **God, please help me worry less and rely on your promises more. Amen.**

Living it out

I say to GOD, "Be my Lord!" Without you, nothing makes sense. « Psalm 16:2 (*The Message*)

Take a sheet of blank paper and cut it into a dozen or so strips. On each slip of paper, write something big or small that causes you anxiety or stress. It can be something as ordinary as "going to the dentist" to something profound like "being afraid I'll die in a car wreck." Use as many slips of paper as you need.

Now take three more pieces of blank paper. On one full sheet write LOW STRESS. On another write MEDIUM STRESS, and on the last paper write HIGH STRESS.

Place the LOW STRESS, MEDIUM STRESS, and HIGH STRESS papers on a large table or on your bed. Now place each of the small stress slips on the appropriate paper. For example, if doing poorly on an important exam is one of your stressors, but it isn't all that important to you, place it on the LOW STRESS paper. If, on the other hand, getting a low grade on an important test is really stressful for you, place the slip on the HIGH STRESS paper.

As we've examined, some stress is inevitable for everyone, but how you react to this stress makes all the difference whether you conquer stress or stress conquers you. Take advantage of God's promises in stressful times. Accept the rest and peace that Jesus offers. Worry less and trust in God more.

Gather all the stressors on your LOW STRESS paper, and begin tearing up the slips of paper as you say this prayer out loud (or silently if you feel more comfortable):

prayer » Jesus, you have promised to lighten my load, to walk alongside me during the tough times. I relinquish to you these stresses in my life. Thank you for your promises. Amen.

Now take all the slips of paper on the MEDIUM STRESS paper and begin to tear them up as you say this prayer:

prayer » Jesus, because you love and care for me, you have invited me to share with you all the things that cause me stress. I'm doing just that. Thank you for being present in my life. Amen.

Finally, take all the slips of paper that represent the HIGH STRESS things in your life. Once again tear these up as you pray this prayer:

prayer » Okay, God, these are the really big stressors in my life. Sometimes they cause me so much anxiety or worry that it is hard for me to function. I know that you will be with me in all my tough times. Accept these torn slips of paper as my acknowledgement of your love and care for me. As today's Scripture says, "Be my Lord! Without you, nothing makes sense." Amen.

IMPORTANT NOTE: Be sure to remember that there may be some medium or high stresses that, in addition to prayer, you need to seek out others for help.

NOTES

1. My condensation and paraphrase of Matthew 6:25-34 and Luke 12:22-34

014
TRAUMA

You, Lord, give true peace to those who depend on you because they trust you.

« Isaiah 26:3 (*NCV*)

Serious illness

Be strong and courageous; do not be frightened or dismayed, for the LORD your God is with you wherever you go. « Joshua 1:9

Shawndra was fourteen years old when she was first diagnosed with cancer. Since that time she has spent more time in a hospital than in high school.

Brad's life began to unravel during his second year of high school. Identified as severely bipolar, neither his teachers nor his classmates have made efforts to understand his mental illness.

God is with you wherever you go

Luis, while coming home from marching band practice, lost control of his car on a patch of black ice and crashed into a concrete embankment. He spent most of his final year of high school in a residential rehab program sixty miles from home.

When it comes to health, most teenagers experience nothing more serious than an occasional cold or episode of flu. But the reality for some youth, like Shawndra, Brad, and Luis, is that they must deal with difficult and complex health issues. Perhaps you are one of them, or you know someone who is. Normal high school concerns, like getting a paper written or finding the perfect prom dress, pale in comparison to what you face on a daily basis.

If you struggle with serious health issues, it takes a lot of courage to be you. You need people in your life who love you and give you support and encouragement, people who take the time to know about your specific health concerns (as much as you want them to know) and are understanding and sympathetic. But when others let you down, which they probably will, always remember that God knows your situation intimately and cares about every aspect of your life. As the Scripture above reminds us, "God is with you wherever you go."

prayer » **God, it is hard being me sometimes. Please send people into my life who build me up, cheer me on, and genuinely care about what my life is like. Give me strength and courage to face whatever comes. Amen.**

Addictions

Be strong and bold. « Deuteronomy 31:6

Any habit that has the power to take total control of one's life physically or emotionally is an addiction. Although we most commonly think of addiction as drug, alcohol, and smoking related, there are a number of other addictions people face: gambling, pornography, sex, food, gaming, and even shopping (overspending).

You might be saying to yourself, I know all that. I've heard this a thousand times! But one beer at a party or one cigarette smoked with a friend or thirty minutes perusing a few porn sites—that seems harmless. After all,

No one sets out to become an addict

the teenage years are all about experimentation, right? Everyone else is trying these things, too, by the way. I'll be able to stop with one snort of crystal meth or one sexual encounter. I just want to know what it's like. Besides, I'm smart, and I know my limits.

No one sets out to become an addict. Most addicts thought they knew their limits and could stop their addictive behavior at any time. That is what makes addiction so insidious and dangerous. You have to be strong, courageous, and gutsy to not give into potentially harmful behaviors that seem fun, make you feel good, and help you belong. Pray for that strength and courage. Find and rely on friends who are interested in being strong and courageous with you.

If you have an addiction, understand that it is a rare person who can end addiction without help. If it takes strength and courage to refrain from addictive behavior in the first place, it takes even more strength and courage to overcome an addiction. Find someone to guide, support, and help you through that difficult journey.

prayer » With your help, I can be strong, courageous, and bold. Amen.

Change

I the LORD do not change. « Malachi 3:6

John's mother tossed his favorite T-shirt in the trash three times. John fished the shirt out of the trash three times. He had acquired the T-shirt on a family vacation when he was thirteen, but his mother doesn't share his appreciation of the shirt. She sees holes and stains; he sees comfort, stability, and good memories.

Change is tough. Even a minor change like giving up a favorite shirt can cause uneasiness, while really big changes—like moving to a new town, experiencing the death of someone close to you, parents divorcing, attending a different school, starting a job, making new friends—can be major anxiety-producing events.

One of the things that make change so difficult is that one change can set into motion a whole lot of other changes, each of which brings its own set of challenges. Imagine a mobile of six colorful little shapes hanging peacefully over a baby's crib. Someone comes along and flicks one of the shapes. The movement of that shape causes the other five shapes to wildly shake and spin. Over time the mobile's unrest slows down and finally stops—all is at peace again.[1]

Grab hold of God's promise of steadiness and stability

Here's what the mobile has to do with change in real life: Let's say your parents decide to divorce (a shape is flicked). Changes in your life and for all the other family members are huge (the entire mobile shakes and spins). Discomfort and unrest continue until a new definition of family life is worked out and the upheaval settles down (the shapes gradually settle into rest). When change is difficult and you need some stability in your life, grab hold of God's promise of steadiness and stability: "I the LORD do not change."

prayer » I need you, God. When things spin out of control around me, I need you. Amen.

Abuse

Give all your worries and cares to God, for [God] cares about what happens to you. « 1 Peter 5:7 (*NLT*)

When it comes to abuse, the statistics are pretty scary. It is possible that you or someone you know has already encountered or will encounter abuse of some kind: physical abuse ranging from fist fights to weapon use, sexual abuse by acquaintances or strangers, bullying that may be physical, verbal, or emotional.

Abuse is never okay. There is no sugar coating or positive spin that makes physical, sexual, emotional, or verbal abuse all right. And contrary to what an abuser may claim, the victim is never responsible for the abuse.

Ideally, you've already discussed the topic of abuse at home, school, and church. Ideally, you are taking measures to keep yourself safe and out of potentially dangerous situations. Ideally, if you have been abused in any way, you have received or are still receiving the assistance you need, and, if not, as soon as you read this you will do so by telling someone you trust, asking for their advice and help.

Abuse is never okay

Jesus experienced verbal abuse during his entire ministry. And talk about violent physical abuse! He was flogged, stripped, beaten, and crucified! If you have been abused, Jesus understands, and he cares. He invites you to share your sorrows, pain, anger, frustrations, and fears with him.

prayer » Jesus, you have promised to walk with me and carry my burdens. Come! Come right now. Thank you. Amen.

Peer pressure

Whoever walks with the wise will become wise; whoever walks with fools will suffer harm. « Proverbs 13:20

If you are like most teens, you struggle between fitting in with your peers, while being your own unique self. As much as you want to be known and appreciated for who you are individually, the tug and pull to be and do what everyone else is being and doing is never greater than in middle school and high school. Peer approval, almost always some unspoken set of rules that makes a person "in" or "out," causes great stress for most teens. Peer pressure is brutal: wear the right clothes; look a certain way; drink, smoke, do drugs, have sex; be smart but not too smart; be thin and physically fit; have a nice car; show off the latest technology; have a boyfriend or girlfriend; go to prom in a limousine; hang with the popular kids; apply to prestigious colleges; go on exotic trips.

I was taking a social studies test in ninth grade when the teacher left the classroom. The girl sitting behind me tapped my shoulder with her pencil and whispered, "Can I copy your answers?" Of course I knew better than to cheat on a test, but here was the most popular girl in the entire ninth grade talking to me and acknowledging that I was smart enough to copy from. I leaned a little to the right and pushed my test paper to the left to give her a clear view of my answers. It was at that moment the teacher returned, and she immediately caught on to what we were doing.

Be smart, be reasonable, and be strong

I got into a lot of trouble both at school and at home, but I learned something valuable from the experience: it's just not worth it to give in to the pressure to do something I know is morally wrong just so that I will be liked. Be smart, be reasonable, and be strong when faced with the pressure of your peers!

prayer » God, I want to be liked and fit in. Yet I want to be honest, true, and comfortable with myself. I need strength not to compromise these two desires. Amen.

DIVE: DEVOTIONS FOR DEEPER LIVING

Family

It is truly wonderful when relatives live together in peace.
« Psalm 133:1 (*CEV*)

When I was a pastor, quite a few parents made their way into my office to talk about how their teens didn't seem to want to spend much time at home, even resisting family outings in order to be with their friends. One parent said, "My daughter's peers have more influence on her than we do; she cares more about their approval than about ours." I was thinking but didn't say out loud, Yes, and what about that isn't normal?

Continue to work on good communication and mutual respect

I felt for them; I had experienced feeling the same way when our daughters were teenagers. But I was also sympathetic to their teens, because the truth is that practicing independence and developing important relationships outside the home is a natural and inevitable part of your growing up. It doesn't mean that you love your family any less or that you no longer need them. (Think about all the ways you still do need them.) It may mean, however, that you sometimes find yourself bristling or clashing with family rules, restrictions, or ideas as you are trying to figure out how to make your own decisions and move into adulthood. Sometimes it might feel like everyone in your family is walking on eggshells, but the important thing is to continue to work on good communication and mutual respect, all the while relying on a whole lot of prayer, grace, and love.

I am assuming that your family life is basically positive, but if your family problems exceed normal teenager and parent conflict, it is important that you find a trusted adult to help you move through the maze of highly difficult family relationships. And if you're not sure how normal your situation is, then talk with someone.

prayer » Sometimes my family just doesn't understand me or accept who I am becoming. God, help us all be patient with each other. Amen.

Living it out

A healthy spirit conquers adversity, but what can you do when the spirit is crushed? « Proverbs 18:14 (*The Message*)

Human beings can withstand most of the challenges and trials that come their way as long as they have hope that things will get better. All the tough things covered in this section (serious illness or disability, addiction, change, abuse, peer pressure, and family dynamics) and all the other troubles that we face in our lives are usually manageable as long as we do not lose hope. I like how the focus Scripture puts it: "A healthy spirit conquers adversity, but what can you do when the spirit is crushed?"

Good question. What can you do when your spirit is crushed? Have you ever felt hopeless? When? What were the circumstances? How did you regain hope? When one loses hope, one has lost almost all ability to keep one's head above water. Some people find hopelessness so overwhelming that they are unable to function, become depressed, and even take their own lives.

One practice that has been helpful to me in overcoming feelings of hopelessness has been to find a Bible verse to recite as a mantra of hope, something to repeat again and again until the message truly sinks into my psyche. I have chosen Romans 15:13 as my Scripture of hope: *"May the God of hope fill you with all joy and peace in believing, so that you may abound in hope by the power of the Holy Spirit."* I've written the verse on a brightly colored piece of cardstock and tucked it in the jewelry drawer of my dresser. I've long since lost track of the number of times I've opened that drawer to read that verse, and the paper is now crumpled and worn.

Look up these Bible verses that have to do with hope.

Psalm 34:18	Isaiah 43:1b-2	Philippians 4:13
Psalm 39:7	Romans 5:3-5	1 Peter 1:21
Psalm 71:5	Romans 8:28	
Psalm 94:19	Romans 15:13	

Choose one of the passages as your Scripture of hope—your "go to" Scripture when you despair and need a little hope. Write it here:

_____
_____
_____
_____
_____
_____
_____
_____
_____
_____
_____
_____
_____
_____
_____
_____
_____
_____

Now rewrite the passage on an index card or piece of heavy paper. Put the paper in a place where you can see it or find it quickly—on your dresser or mirror, in your nightstand drawer, locker, or backpack. Consider memorizing it for even quicker access to the promise of hope that the Scripture offers.

When needed, refer to the Scripture, reading or repeating it from memory over and over again until it becomes your very own believed words of hope. God is a God of hope. Jesus Christ offers us the promise of hope now and forever.

NOTES

1. Clara L. Gaff and Carma L. Byland, eds., *Family Communication About Genetics: Theory and Practice.* (New York: Oxford University Press USA, 2010), 105.

015
DEALING WITH DEATH AND DYING

For everything there is a season, and a time for every matter under heaven: a time to be born, and a time to die. « Ecclesiastics 3:1-2

God's presence in life and death

The LORD is near to the brokenhearted. « Psalm 34:18

You have probably experienced the death of a favorite pet, an older neighbor, or a great-uncle. Perhaps you have also had a more intimate relationship with death in the loss of a parent, grandparent, sibling, or close friend.

What does it feel like to die? What happens immediately after death? Is there really an afterlife? Why do people fear death? Why does it hurt so much to lose someone? Will I ever be happy again after someone I love has died? What do you say to a person who is dying? How do you relate to a person whose close family member is dying or has died? Why does God let people you love die?

Death is as natural as birth

If we remove all personal connection to death for a moment, we understand that death is as natural as birth. We all are born; we live; we die. So if death is inevitable and part of God's creation plan, why does it cause so much emotional pain? Why are we so brokenhearted?

As followers of Jesus, we look at all these questions through that lens. As painful as it is when someone we deeply love dies, we do not need to fear death. We can dislike it, dread it, and want to postpone it—sure! But fear death? Not with the hope of resurrection and the promise that even though we walk through the dark valley of death, we are not alone.[1]

prayer » Thank you, Jesus, for being with me through life and death. Amen.

It hurts when someone dies

[David wept and said,] "O my son, Absalom, my son, my son Absalom! Would I had died instead of you. O Absalom, my son, my son!" « 2 Samuel 18:33

David's poignant cries of grief over the death of his son, Absalom, mirror our sadness and tears when someone we love dies. Our daughters were eighteen and sixteen when their grandfather died. They were very close to my parents and over the years spent a great deal of time at their condo, only a few blocks from our house. Grandpa was their cheerleader, mentor, friend, and confidant. Only in his seventies, we had anticipated many more wonderful years with Grandpa. But one morning in late November he had a stroke while doing his morning exercises and died a few days later.

'Tis better to have loved and lost than never to have loved at all

One of our daughters told me, "I wish I hadn't loved Grandpa so much; then his dying wouldn't hurt so badly." She was right about one thing: the death of someone you love hurts deeply. But she was mistaken that the absence of her intense pain would have been a good trade-off for the loving relationship she had with her grandfather. (Of course, she knew that.) Alfred Lord Tennyson expressed this beautifully in a poetic tribute to a well-loved friend after his unexpected death: "'Tis better to have loved and lost than never to have loved at all."[2]

There is no way *under*, *over*, or *around* the pain and sadness that accompany the death of someone who is well loved. The only path is *through* the pain. The route one takes is personal, and grief will travel at its own speed and on its own timetable. Time will eventually begin to heal the stabbing, fresh, and poignant pain of losing someone you love, while good memories and the joy of loving and having been loved will always remain.

prayer » Comfort me, Lord, when someone I love dies. I thank you for the love we shared. In the name of Jesus who cried at the death of his close friend, Amen.

How long until I feel better?

Blessed are those who mourn, for they will be comforted.
« Matthew 5:4

My father's funeral was the day before Thanksgiving. On the way home from the service, I had to stop at the grocery store to pick up a few things for dinner for the twenty family members who were staying at our house. All around me were families choosing food for their Thanksgiving feasts, laughing and enjoying each other's company. Right in the middle of the produce aisle, I burst into tears. Didn't they realize that there was nothing to be happy about; didn't they know that the world had forever changed? If you have experienced the death of someone you love, you might identify with me crying in the grocery store. To the one grieving it appears that everyone else is going on with life as usual without recognizing that you are trying to find a new "normal."

I was surprised that my sadness lasted such a long time

I was surprised that my sadness lasted such a long time. Grief would come flooding over me at the most unexpected times. I was confused by my grief when it took so many turns. It helped, however, to revisit the five stages of grief that most of us go through when we lose someone we love: denial, anger, bargaining, depressions, and acceptance.[3] It was good to be reminded that we do not pass through the stages in an orderly or quick manner but jump back and forth between them, staying an unpredictable amount of time in each stage.

The most important thing I learned is that whatever stage of grief I was experiencing I was not alone. I was picked up and carried through my sadness by good and caring friends. I was picked up and carried by Jesus, who himself was well acquainted with grief. I was able to share with Jesus about how much I missed my father and, later, my mother. Jesus never minded my tears; Jesus never grew tired of my stories and was patient with me when I was stuck in grief.

prayer » When I am sad, I will depend on you for comfort. Thank you for carrying me through the tough times, Jesus. Amen.

Why do tragedies happen?

God is our refuge and strength, a very present help in trouble. « Psalm 46:1

It was homecoming, and after school two boys went to the carwash. They washed and waxed the car and then swept the inside to make sure their dates' dresses wouldn't get dirty. But they never made it to the dance. On their way home from the carwash, a speeding driver who had been drinking steadily for hours rear-ended the boys. They were killed instantly.

I taught at the school the boys attended and was a friend of one of their mothers. In fact, I sang at her son's funeral. Upon my arrival at the church on the morning of the service, she hugged me and said only one thing, "Why?"

There it is—the universal question when horrible things happen: Why? Intellectually we know that bad things happen to good people, but why doesn't God stop those bad things from happening? Isn't God powerful enough? Asking the "why?" question will be one of the most natural things you do whenever you face difficult circumstances, especially the death of someone you love. Usually the only answer to "why?", given our limited earthly understanding is "I don't know."

We can be assured that God is present in our grief

Sometimes tragedy comes because others impose it upon humanity (for example, the Holocaust). Sometimes tragedy comes from poor choices we make (for example, choosing to smoke heavily and consequently contracting lung cancer). But most of the time tragedy comes about as the unavoidable coincidences of life (for example, the boys going home from the carwash and being in the wrong place at the wrong time). We may never understand why something happens, but we can be assured that God is present in our grief and a source of great comfort. That is God's promise: "I will be your refuge, your strength, and your help in troubled times."

prayer » Be with me, Lord, when I face my death or the death of someone I love. Be my refuge and my strength. Amen.

The hope of heaven

In my Father's house there are many dwelling places. If it were not so, would I have told you that I go to prepare a place for you? And if I go and prepare a place for you, I will come again and will take you to myself, so that where I am, there you may be also. « John 14:2-3

The person delivering the eulogy at the funeral of a wonderful man said, "Enjoy your loved ones while you can because when they are gone, it's over." Those of us who take Jesus' words seriously believe otherwise, of course.

I cannot imagine facing my own death or the death of someone I deeply care about without the hope of heaven, where we will spend eternity in the presence of Jesus, reunite with those we love, be freed from tears and suffering, and experience total peace and joy.

Death has been swallowed up in victory

In the little book of Titus, we read, "We . . . become heirs according to the hope of eternal life."[4] Our hope in the midst of intense pain and loss is that this earthly life is not the end. We will see our loved ones again. Death is not something to fear; "death has been swallowed up in victory."[5]

When Jesus predicted his death at the Passover meal with his disciples, they were confused and saddened. Going away? Where? Why? Could they go, too? His answer includes these timeless words of comfort: "I will see you again, and your hearts will rejoice, and no one will take your joy from you."[6]

prayer » Thank you for the promise of eternal life, God. In the name of the one who promises us peace and joy in our heavenly home, Amen.

How can I help?

Help carry each other's burdens. In this way you will follow Christ's teachings. « Galatians 6:2 (*GWT*)

Many people are unsure of what to do or say to people who are dying or who have lost a loved one. Since you will someday face this situation, thinking about it ahead of time will help make the experience far less intimidating. Here are some tips:

- Don't worry about saying the "right" thing to a person who is dying or grieving. There is nothing you can say to make things right anyway. If you are able to say nothing more than "I'm so sorry," that is enough.
- Avoid talking down to the grieving one in such words as "I know how you feel" or "he (she) is better off with God" or "this is God's will." None of us really knows how someone else feels, and assuming to know what God's will is a bit presumptuous.
- Far more important than your words is your presence. You might prefer to stay away from a painful or uncomfortable situation, but resist that temptation and be present.
- If the dying or grieving want to talk, be sure to listen, listen, listen.
- A hug or a soft squeeze on a hand or arm can meaningfully replace spoken words.
- Don't be afraid of crying or being emotional in front of the dying or grieving.
- Doing something tangible for the dying or grieving is literally "carrying each other's burdens." Mow their lawn, weed their garden, pick up groceries, bake brownies, offer childcare, read Scripture or a favorite book, etc.

> *Don't worry about saying the "right" thing to a person who is dying or grieving*

- Send a card to someone who is dying and mention something you appreciate about the person.
  Send a card to the family of someone who has died and tell how their loved one has had an impact on your life. Better yet, send several cards and space them out over a period of time.
- Realize that people who are dying or grieving are sometimes not quite themselves. Be gracious and forgiving if they say or do something strange and unusual.

prayer » I pray for those I know who are dying or grieving. With your help, I can be a good burden carrier. Amen.

Living it out

And God will wipe away every tear from their eyes.
« Revelation 7:17

Fear of the unknown is unsettling and uncomfortable. However, the more information we gather and the more we understand something, the less we fear it. This is true about death. Much of what we might fear can be explored with people who are trained or knowledgeable about the dying process. The first project will help you do just that.

Option One
INTERVIEW PEOPLE IN THE KNOW.

If you would like more information and help in understanding the actual physical process of death, contact a doctor or nurse you know to talk to about what physically happens to a dying person. To help you get started, you might ask: What are the signs that death is near? Is dying painful? How do you know when you should continue to work to save a life and when it is time for nature to take its course? What happens to the physical body once a person dies?

If you would like more information and help in understanding what the Bible says about death, eternal life, and heaven, contact your pastor to talk about these things. If you currently do not have a pastor, call a pastor that someone you know recommends and ask for a few minutes of the pastor's time. Go to the interview with prepared questions; for example: What does the Bible say about heaven? How does one know that he/she will have eternal life? What happens to a soul after dying? Will I see my loved ones again?

If you would like more information and help in understanding the emotional aspects of dying, contact someone you know who has lost a family member or close friend. Prepare some questions before you meet: Were you with the person when she/he died? If so, what was that like? Was it scary? If you were not present, do you wish you had been there? Why or why not? How did you feel right after the death? What were the things people said to you after the death that were helpful or comforting? What things did they say that were not helpful? Do you think you have gone through any stages of grief? If so, and if you don't mind, would you tell me about that? Is there any advice you can give me on how to face the death of someone I love?

Option Two
EXPLORE THE STORY OF LAZARUS'S DEATH.

1. Read the story in John 11:1-44.

2. What is the reaction of Mary and Martha to their brother's death? The disciples' reaction? Jesus' reaction?

_____

_____

_____

_____

_____

_____

_____

_____

_____

3. If you have experienced the death of someone you know well, were your reactions similar to the characters' reactions in the story? Do these characters give you any insights into how to handle the death of someone you love?

_____

_____

_____

_____

_____

_____

_____

_____

_____

NOTES

1. Psalm 23:4
2. Alfred Lord Tennyson, "In Memoriam XXVII," *Poetry for Young People* (New York: Sterling Publishers, 2003), 31.
3. Elizabeth Kubler-Ross, *On Death and Dying* (New York: Macmillan Publishing, 1969), 34-121.
4. Titus 3:7
5. 1 Corinthians 15:54
6. John 16:22

016
MAKING DECISIONS

We know all things work together for good for those who love God.

« Romans 8:28

Decide what kind of decision-maker you are

Trust in the LORD with all your heart, and do not rely on your own insight. In all your ways acknowledge [God], and [the Lord] will make straight your paths. « Proverbs 3:5-6

You do not need to fly solo and rely just on your own understanding

Every day we make many decisions. Some are about little matters: whether to have a bagel or toast for breakfast; which shirt to wear, the blue one or the red one. Other decisions are more significant: whether to mark A, B, C, or D on a multiple choice history test; what friends to invite to your birthday party. Still other decisions carry great impact and lasting importance: which college to attend, who to marry, what career to pursue, whether to become a follower of Jesus.

How would you describe yourself?
- Someone who finds decision-making fairly easy; a quick decision-maker.
- Someone who can't make up his or her mind and keeps going back and forth on a decision; a waffler.
- Someone who makes a decision but continues to wonder if it was the correct one; a second-guesser.
- Someone who takes a long time to make decisions, always fearing a poor or wrong choice; an agonizer.
- Someone who can float between being a quick decision-maker; a waffler, a second-guesser, or an agonizer.

Good decision-making relies on wisdom, practice, good sense, and clear priorities. But you do not need to fly solo and rely just on your own understanding when making a decision. Good decision-making is enhanced by reliance on God and the counsel of other people.

prayer » Help me grow in my ability to make wise decisions by relying on my own skills, seeking the input of others, and trusting in God. In Jesus' name, Amen.

Pray about your choices

If any of you is lacking in wisdom, ask God, who gives to all generously and ungrudgingly, and it will be given you. « James 1:5

Wisdom is a key ingredient to making good decisions. Perhaps you have assumed that wisdom belongs only to gray-haired men and women who have lived a long, full life. According to James, wisdom is available for all of us. We just need to ask God for it.

God says to the Old Testament prophet Jeremiah, "Call to me and I will answer you, and will tell you great and hidden things that you have not known."[1] Why limp along using only our own limited understanding when God has promised to let us in on "great and hidden things"?

As you pray for wisdom and the ability to make good decisions, believe and expect an answer to your prayers. It would be nice if God's help would come in the form of a giant billboard along the roadside or behind one of those planes that pulls message streamers; something like: "Maria, go to XYZ University" or "Josh, you should be a chef!"

Unfortunately, you likely will not hear from God through personal messages on billboards or streamers in the sky. How then? With gentle nudges of the Holy Spirit that keep particular thoughts in the forefront of your mind; with advice you find in Scripture, sermon, or song; with counsel you receive from people you trust.

Believe and expect an answer to your prayers

prayer » I want to know the "great and hidden things" you have in mind for me, God. I pray for wisdom. I pray for guidance. I pray in Jesus' name and with the expectation of an answer. Amen.

Hear the Bible

Your word is a lamp to my feet and a light to my path.
« Psalm 119:105

I may have the world's worst sense of direction. A friend likes to joke: "Whichever way Cindy says to turn, go the opposite direction and you'll be headed the right way." I need a GPS or map to get from point A to point B in all new situations. The Bible is like a compass, map, or GPS for our life. A book written thousands of years ago is still relevant for the twenty-first century. God's Word, the Bible, is a lamp that can illumine our way when we have significant decisions to make. Although Scripture may not speak directly to all our important decisions, it is surprisingly helpful in many situations. Here is one:

Tomeka, seventeen, was tired of saying no to drinking when her friends gathered for weekend parties. Everyone was drinking! What could it hurt? Maybe she should just go ahead and join them.

The Bible is a lamp that can illumine our way

Tomeka turned to Scripture to help her make a decision about drinking and found two verses. The first was from 1 Corinthians 6:19-20 (*NLT*): "Your body is the temple of the Holy Spirit, . . . honor God with your body." She concluded that underage drinking did not treat her body as any kind of temple. Getting drunk would certainly not honor God by any stretch of the imagination.

The second verse told her: "Let every person be subject to the governing authorities" (Rom 13:1). Since drinking as a minor is illegal (even if a whole lot of other teens are doing it), how could she do it in good conscience?

prayer » I know your holy Word can guide me, but for that to happen, I need to read and study it more to know what it actually says. With good intentions to do so, I pray in Jesus' name. Amen.

Use your head

The clever consider their steps. « Proverbs 14:15

Sometimes a decision is between something moral and something immoral, but more often our decisions are between two or more *good* things. Decision-making becomes more difficult when there seems to be no right or wrong answer, no clear front-runner.

Zach had applied for several summer jobs. On the same day, he received job offers for the two positions he wanted the most: lifeguard at the local city pool and lifeguard at a summer camp. He did not know how he was going to choose between the two great opportunities, so he made two poster board charts. On the left side of one chart he wrote, LOCAL JOB—PROS, and on the right side he wrote LOCAL JOB—CONS. He did the same on the other poster: CAMP JOB—PROS on the left side, CAMP JOB—CONS on the right side. Over the next several days, Zach wrote down on both charts every reason he could think of that made each job a good choice or not a good choice. To his surprise, once he analyzed all the things he had written down on both sides of the charts, it was fairly clear to him that the local lifeguarding job was the better choice for that summer.

> *Decision-making becomes more difficult when there seems to be no right or wrong answer*

It is possible that Zach would have been happy in either job, but because of his careful deliberation and well-thought-out approach to decision-making, he absolutely felt he had made the right decision. He had no need to second-guess himself all summer and continually revisit the question: What if I had taken the other job?

prayer » Thank you, God for the ability to look at all sides of a question. Thanks, too, for the peace of mind that descends when I've used my decision-making abilities in careful and logical ways. Amen.

Ask others for counsel

Without counsel, plans go wrong, but with many advisors they succeed. « Proverbs 15:22

One of the signs of mature decision-making is asking for help when you need it. We can ask God, of course, but God often speaks through people who can enter into our decision-making.

Maria's parents were concerned that her plans to participate in two spring sports would make it difficult to get the grades she needed to obtain college scholarships. Further, both of Maria's coaches wanted her to concentrate only on their sport, either track and field or softball. She knew she needed to choose between the two, but she enjoyed both of the sports and was talented in each. The decision weighed heavily on her mind, and she seemed unable to make a decision by herself.

God often speaks through people who can enter into our decision-making

Maria asked her cousin Jose and two close friends, Ashley and Shirushi, to mull over the decision with her. She requested that they ask probing questions and to stick with her until she had a clear decision. They agreed, and the four teens met at her house on a Saturday afternoon. Jose, Ashley, and Shirushi asked Maria what she most enjoyed about each sport. They asked her to reflect on which one she felt she was better at. Jose wondered if one sport has a greater potential to earn her a scholarship. Ashley asked whether she enjoyed an individual or team sport more. Shirushi asked Maria which coach taught her the most.

They quizzed her about what sport would serve her well throughout life, after her competing days were over. They inquired about which sport she would miss the most if she suddenly found it absent from her life. Jose wanted to know which sport she thought about more often. The trio continued to ask questions and to reflect on Maria's answers, and after a few hours, the foursome came to the conclusion that she should devote her time to track and field. A sense of peace and calm for the first time in weeks came over Maria.[2]

prayer » Thank you, God, for people I can trust to help in my decision-making. In Jesus' name, Amen.

Figure out what is important

You cannot serve God and wealth. « Matthew 6:24

As you get further along in your schooling and as your life experiences expand, you will begin thinking about what kind of career you would enjoy someday. This decision is going to be based on your talents, interests, and job market, of course, but I'm guessing that salary or potential earning power might also be fairly high on your list of considerations.

I know a youth pastor who, after careful observation, believed that a young man in her youth group would make a wonderful minister. He was outgoing, articulate, compassionate, and faith-filled. One evening after youth group, on a night when he had led a meaningful and well-prepared Bible study, she talked to him about her observation. He thanked her for her confidence in him but said, "I don't think I could ever be a pastor. There's just not enough money in it for me."

Consider refraining from using money or prestige as strong reasons to do something

Another youth, toying with a career in advertising or nursing, knew she likely had talents that could be used in either field. Trying hard to set aside consideration of salary and what anyone else thought she should do, she carefully decided that God's will for her was to go into advertising.

When making an important life decision, consider refraining from using money or prestige as strong reasons to do something or not to do something. As tempting as money and prestige might be, there are other significant factors for followers of Jesus to consider. What is God's will for your life? What career will allow you to be the "servant" that Jesus talks about? What will bring you deep personal contentment and happiness?

prayer » Guide me, God, in looking at career options that are based more on serving you than on salary or prestige. Amen.

Living it out

Whoever finds [wisdom] finds life. « Proverbs 8:35

In this exercise, you will work on your good decision-making skills. Follow the steps below and reflect on the experience.

Step One

Identify a decision that you need to make. This can be any kind of decision, but choose something that is not too long term or time consuming for practice purposes. Write down what needs to be decided.

_____

_____

_____

_____

_____

_____

_____

Step Two

Identify at least two choices you have to decide between. If there are more than two choices, list those as well.

_____

_____

_____

_____

_____

_____

_____

Step Three

Spend time in prayer, asking God to help you in your decision-making so that you have a clear answer and direction. Search the Bible for pertinent Scriptures that help point you in the right direction.

Step Four

Choose an option below to further help you arrive at a decision.

1. Make a chart for each of your choices. Add a PROS column and a CONS column on each chart. Take several days to write all the reasons for a particular choice (PRO) and all the reasons not to choose that option (CON).

2. Ask several people who know you well to gather and help in your decision-making. Encourage them to question you, gently push and prod you, and to stick with it until the entire group and you feel like you've collectively arrived at the best decision.

Step Five

Reflect on this decision-making experience. Were you successful in making a decision? What was it like to use the process you chose? Do you think it was easier or more difficult to make a decision in such a deliberate way? Do you think you would use this same process again? Why or why not?

_____

_____

_____

_____

_____

_____

_____

_____

NOTES:

1. Jeremiah 33:3
2. This method of decision-making is called The Clearness Committee, a practice commonly used by the Society of Friends (Quakers).

017
JUSTICE FOR ALL

Maintain justice, and do what is right, for soon my salvation will come, and my deliverance be revealed. « Isaiah 56:1

Love your neighbor—including your enemy

You shall love your neighbor as yourself. « Matthew 22:39

In our key verse, Jesus is obviously using the word *neighbor* more broadly than just the person who lives next door. He means to encompass all humanity: the man at the end of your street, the girl sitting next to you in biology class, the trucker in Houston, the actress in New York City, the street beggar in Delhi, the farmer in Tanzania, and the teenage rickshaw driver in Beijing.

Think of your neighbor as no different than yourself

This is an easy commandment to keep if you like the girl sitting next to you in biology class or do not know the farmer in Tanzania and likely never will. It's not so easy when you do not like your neighbor. Jesus knew we would find some of our neighbors more difficult to love than others, but he makes it pretty clear that we cannot pick and choose whom to love: "If you love those who love you, what credit is that to you? For even sinners love those who love them."[1]

Each of us is equally lovable in the sight of God, even those people we do not like, people we might even call our enemies. Jesus identifies loving our neighbors as much as we love ourselves as the second most important commandment, second only to loving God with our whole being.[2] So, how do we go about keeping this commandment? One way is to pray. Loving people whom we do not like is hard work, and, frankly, sometimes we could use divine intervention. Prayer can open a little crack in our hearts that allows us to begin seeing someone in a new and different light: to see them as Jesus sees them, someone worth loving.

Another way to work on this commandment is to think of your neighbor as no different than yourself, someone with a family, with financial and health struggles, with desires and needs, with joys and sadness—just like you. Humanizing and personalizing a neighbor helps us begin to see all people in a new light.

prayer » God, it is easy to love those who love me, but not so easy to love someone I do not like. Help me find a way to see others as you see them. Thank you for loving me. Amen.

DIVE: DEVOTIONS FOR DEEPER LIVING

Treat others as you want to be treated

Do to others as you would have them do to you. « Luke 6:31

Perhaps there are no more powerful eleven words than the Golden Rule: "Do to others as you would have them do to you." If all people across the globe took these words of Jesus seriously, the course of history would be forever altered. As great as that dream is, however, we really have no control over others living by these profound words—only over ourselves.

Here are a few examples of following the Golden Rule on a personal and practical level:

- Talking to your parents with a respectful attitude, *because* that is how you want them to talk to you.
- Being patient with a slow and inexperienced cashier, *because* you hope that when you are on your first day of a new job the customers or your coworkers will be patient with you.
- Slowing your car to let someone pull out from her driveway onto a busy street, *because* you know that you were late for school last week since no one would let you pull out into traffic.
- Supporting your friend, even if his or her bad mood is annoying, *because* you will certainly be in a bad mood at some time in the future.
- Refusing to bully, tease, or taunt a student at school, *because* you know you would never want to be treated like that.
- Returning a twenty dollar bill to the girl who dropped it from her wallet while getting a lunch ticket, *because* you know that you would be upset if you lost that much money.
- Treating your date with respect, *because* you know that you want to be treated with respect.

If everyone took these words seriously, history would be forever altered

prayer » God, I know it won't always be easy, but help me make it my daily motto to "do to others what I would like them to do to me." Amen.

Get rid of "isms"

There is no longer Jew or Greek, there is no longer slave or free, there is no longer male and female; for all of you are one in Christ Jesus. « Galatians 3:28

Any time anyone is treated unfairly, improperly, unjustly, and unkindly due to one's race, age, sex, ethnicity, socioeconomic status, disability, sexual orientation, or any other reason, we dishonor God and all of God's creation.

Boldly stand up to the injustices you see around you

Christians must be on the front lines of treating all people equally well. If we follow the Scriptures to love others as ourselves and treat others like we want to be treated, prejudice, bias, hatred, and superiority have no place in our lives.

Following Jesus means working against the "isms" you come in contact with: racism, ageism, sexism, nationalism, classism, you-name-it-ism! Do not laugh at or participate in jokes or situations that demean others. Refrain from making decisions about people based on what they look like, their intellectual abilities, their age, where they come from, or how much money they have.

Boldly stand up to the injustices you see around you. Be kind and welcoming to all people. It will not be easy, and you may be ridiculed for your stance. But you have the words of Jesus to spur you on: "Love each other in the same way that I have loved you. By showing this kind of love, you declare that you are my followers."[3]

prayer » Jesus, give me the courage and compassion to love all people, to love them because you loved them first. Let me take that stance boldly, even when it is unpopular or suspect. I boldly follow you, Jesus! Amen.

Adjust your relationship with water

If they are thirsty, give them water to drink.
« Proverbs 25:21

This morning I made coffee, gulped down my vitamin pill, took a shower, and did two loads of laundry before heading out the door. Not once did I think about the water I was using to do those tasks.

Thank God for clean, plentiful water

I asked a teenager to chart his water consumption in a typical day. His report:

> I showered in the morning for thirteen minutes; filled a bottle with water for the day, but finished it by fourth period at school; took a few gulps of water from the water fountain before lunch; refilled the water bottle at lunch; took a quick two-to-three minute shower after sixth hour PE class; drank three more bottles of water during and after cross country practice; took a twenty minute shower at home; drank a glass of water with dinner; brushed my teeth with water; and drank two glasses of water before going to bed.

For much of the world, such easy access to fresh, safe, and plentiful water would be an enormous luxury, and in many cases an impossibility. Inadequate and unsafe water bring drought and famine, disease and death.

- One in eight people worldwide lack access to safe water.
- Every twenty seconds a child dies somewhere in the world due to a water-related illness.
- A North American taking a five-minute shower uses more water than a person in a developing country might use in an entire day.[4]

What can you do about this injustice? Thank God for clean, plentiful water. Become aware of your own water consumption. Is there something that needs to be changed? Find reputable organizations that focus on water issues around the world, and become educated, perhaps donating time or money.

prayer » I thank you for clean, safe, and plentiful water, and I pray for those in the world who, at this very moment, are thirsty. Amen.

Make peace

Blessed are the peacemakers, for they will be called children of God. « Matthew 5:9

Once the family of Jake Epp was settled on their new farm, they were eager to meet their nearest neighbor, Ben Strobel. However, that eagerness soon faded as Ben was rude and unfriendly at every turn. His cattle, allowed to graze freely on the Epp's land, trampled their vegetable garden and ruined their first crop of wheat. The Epps tried reasoning with Ben but he replied sarcastically, "If you don't like my cattle on your land, build a fence!" Finally, the Epp family found no other alternative and erected a fence with borrowed money. Not really expecting a fence, Ben was enraged and yelled at the Epps, "This is a free country and my cattle should be able to go wherever they want!"

This is a free country and my cattle should be able to go wherever they want!

Ben's belligerent and abusive behavior continued until the day he suddenly became so ill he was hospitalized. Jake, upon hearing of Ben's grave condition, organized the neighbors to help plant Ben's fields and take care of his animals. The Epp family began visiting Ben in the hospital despite his cranky reception. Each time he was transferred to a different facility because of his worsening condition, the Epp family followed there, too.

Eventually Ben recovered and was able to return home. He found his farm well cared for, the cattle thriving, and his crops growing tall. Jake came to welcome Ben home, and Ben asked, "Why would you do all this for me when I have treated you so badly?" Jake picked up a dusty Bible he saw on Ben's bookshelf and replied, "Because of this!"[5]

prayer » **I want to be a peacemaker, too, God. Even when it would be easier and more satisfying to retaliate, fill me with the desire to be a peacemaker. In the name of the Prince of Peace, Amen.**

Take care of God's earth

The earth is the LORD's and all that is in it, the world, and those who live in it. « Psalm 24:1

As I was riding my bike on a lovely spring afternoon, the passenger in a passing car threw a bag of trash out the window, narrowly missing me. A jogger immediately ran into the road and picked up the scattered contents of the sack and threw the garbage into a nearby trashcan. One of the characters in this vignette was a sixteen-year-old teen and one was a forty-year-old man. Who do you think was the helpful trash-picker-upper? If you guessed the sixteen-year-old, you would be correct.

Look for little ways to make a difference

Many young people have caught the vision that this magnificent earth needs looking after. I have been impressed and humbled by the knowledge many youth have about the environment and their commitment to caring for God's creation. That gives much hope to those of us who are concerned about the world we are leaving for future generations.

What things are you doing in your small corner of the world to honor God's magnificent creation? Look for little ways to make a difference. For example, several middle school youth at my church formed an environmental club and gave it the ambitious name of Save the World Club. Project by project they do whatever they can to encourage the congregation to care for the earth. A high school student, instead of receiving any presents for his birthday, asked for money so he could purchase and plant a tree. Another high schooler made a variety of gift bags from scraps of fabric she found, replacing her family's need to purchase wrapping paper. One church youth group adopted two miles of a busy county road, and routinely picked up trash and planted flowers and bushes along the roadside.

What great ideas do you have for practicing earth care?

prayer » God, thank you for the beauty of this earth. I will do my part to honor your creation. In the name of Jesus I pray. Amen.

Living it out

If you offer your food to the hungry and satisfy the needs of the afflicted, then your light shall rise in the darkness and your gloom be like the noonday. « Isaiah 58:10

Every day 852 million people go hungry.[6] In the United States hunger is a reality for one in every six people,[7] and in Canada over forty percent of all food pantry clients are children.[8]

I hope you have never been hungry. Not the "Mom, I'm starving! What is there to eat?" hunger that comes after a long day at school, but real gut-wrenching hunger; the kind of hunger where you can't concentrate in school; the kind of hunger where you become gravely ill; the kind of hunger that we, as followers of Jesus, should tirelessly work to eliminate.

For this week's "Living it out" project choose one of the following hunger-related activities:

1. Find a food pantry in your community via the Internet, phone book, or church office. Contact the pantry and volunteer in any way they suggest. To make the experience more helpful to the agency, ask if you can bring a friend or two with you. Work at whatever tasks you are given with joy and gratitude.
2. Either by yourself or with some friends, organize a bake sale. Ask permission to sell the goodies at church, school, or some other creative venue. Donate the proceeds from the sale to Heifer International, an agency that sends chickens, goats, cows, and other animals to help alleviate worldwide hunger.
3. Plan a "can party" for your next birthday. Ask everyone you invite to not bring presents, but instead bring nonperishable items that can be given to local food shelters or your church.
4. Plan a "Let's Feed a Family Scavenger Hunt" and take all the gathered food to your church's food pantry, to school for an administrator to distribute to families in need, or to a local food pantry. Details for the scavenger hunt can be found in the Notes.[9]
5. Explore opportunities that are available in your area for community gardens. Participate in existing programs that teach others to grow their own food, or find out how to start such a program. Alternatively, plant your own garden and find ways to distribute your fresh produce.

Reflect

Which project did you choose? Why? When you have completed the project, write down the answers to the following questions. Did anyone work with you on the project? To whom did you give the proceeds? Why did you choose that person or agency? Did you learn anything new about hunger? Do you think what you learned or experienced will affect you in the future?

_____

_____

_____

_____

_____

_____

_____

_____

_____

_____

_____

_____

_____

_____

_____

_____

_____

_____

_____

_____

_____

_____

NOTES

1. Luke 6:32-33
2. Matthew 22:36-40
3. John 13:34-35 (my paraphrase)
4. "Water Facts," http://water.org/learn-about-the-water-crisis/facts/
5. Cornelia Lehn, "Why Are You Doing This for Me?" in *Peace Be with You* (Newton, Kansas: Faith and Life Press, 1980), 110-111.
6. World Vision, "Statistics on Hunger and Poverty," http://www.worldvision.org/resources.nsf/main/Hunger_Statistics.pdf/$file/Hunger_Statistics.pdf
7. "Hunger in America," http://feedingamerica.org/hunger-in-america.aspx
8. "Hunger and Food Security in Canada," http://www.mealexchange.com/index.php?option=com_content&task=view&id=40&Itemid=74#hungerincanada

9. Let's Feed a Family Scavenger Hunt

This scavenger hunt is a good youth group activity or a fun and creative party for eight or more friends. Together the entire group creates a simple menu of three nutritious meals and one snack for a family of four. Write down everything that would be needed to prepare the meals and snack and make several copies of the list. Divide the whole group into smaller groups of two to four people, making sure there is a car and driver for each group. Set a time for all participants to return (at least two hours) and distribute the menu/ingredient list and empty grocery sacks to each small group.

The object is for each group to obtain as many of the items from the menu/ingredient list as possible. How the food is gathered is up to each group: buy the ingredients with their own money, ask stores to donate items, go from house to house and ask for things, etc. Impress on the groups that if they ask for donations they need to explain that all the food collected will be distributed to a local agency concerned with hunger issues.

When groups return at the end of the allotted time, determine which group best completed the assignment and award prizes to each group. The group finding the most items receives a large bag of rice. Second place gets a slightly smaller bag of rice; third place a bit smaller bag of rice, and so on—decreasing the size of the bag of rice for each prize. All groups then add their prizes to the other collected items. Deliver the food to a local agency that works to feed your community's hungry.

018
SERVING OTHERS

As for me and my household, we will serve the LORD. « Joshua 24:15

You can't separate faith and service

What good is it, my brothers and sisters, if you say you have faith but do not have works? Can faith save you? If a brother or sister is naked and lacks daily food, and one of you says to them, "Go in peace; keep warm and eat your fill," and yet you do not supply their bodily needs, what is the good of that? « James 2:14-16

How can we make the world a better place to live? Just because we are young and have little money or time, it does not mean we can't do something.

It is easy to find excuses that justify our hesitancy to step away from our own personal agendas into the world of needs around us. But Christians young or old do not get to choose whether they will serve others or not. Scripture shows that faith and serving others go hand-in-hand. If we are people of faith, we serve.

If we are people of faith, we serve

Jesus tells his disciples that when they feed the hungry, give water to the thirsty, welcome the stranger, clothe the naked, care for the sick, and visit the prisoner, they are doing those things for him. The disciples are confused and ask Jesus, "But when did we ever see you hungry, thirsty, alone, naked, sick, or in prison?" Jesus has a brilliant and challenging answer both for the disciples and for us: "When you take care of those around you, no matter who it is that needs your help, it is as if you are doing those exact same things for me."[1]

prayer » Jesus, give me a servant's heart. Show me ways that I can make this world a better place. Trusting in your presence, I ask this in your name. Amen.

The first will be last and the last will be first

[Jesus said,] "Whoever wants to be first must be last of all and servant of all." « Mark 9:35

There is a folktale about a topsy-turvy world where fish wear leashes and dogs live in the ocean, where flowers go on flagpoles and flags grow on stems, where blueberries are orange and oranges are blue. Some of the things Jesus said must have sounded topsy-turvy, too. Turn the other cheek when someone hits you;[2] love and pray for your enemies;[3] attend to the log in your own eye before pointing out the speck in your neighbor's eye.[4]

The focus Scripture above must have puzzled most of Jesus' listeners as well. The first will be last and the last will be first? The first must be the servant of all?

Jesus demonstrates this mixed-up hierarchy many times. He, the Master, stoops to wash the feet of those who should be washing his feet.[5] He chooses the crooked tax collector, Zacchaeus, for a dinner companion rather than the prestigious and powerful religious authorities.[6] The widow's small offering is praised over the large contributions of the Pharisees.[7] Young people, in a society that greatly discounted the importance of children, are lifted up as examples and models of who will enter the kingdom of heaven.[8] In Jesus' parable, the beggar, Lazarus, ends up in heaven, and the rich man in hell.[9]

We are never too good, too busy, too important, or too holy to serve others

The first shall be last and the last shall be first—this is a good principle to remember as we serve others in the name of Jesus. We are never too good, too busy, too important, or too holy to serve others. There is no act of service beneath us, and we dare not make value judgments as to who or what deserves our help. Humility, kindness, compassion, and unselfishness are the marks of being in last place, which, of course, is really first place in God's kingdom.

prayer » God, this first and last business is unsettling and so counter-cultural. Help me see that in my willingness to humbly serve others I am truly following Jesus. Amen.

Look to the interests of others

Do nothing from selfish ambition or conceit, but in humility regard others as better than yourselves. Let each of you look not to your own interests, but to the interests of others. « Philippians 2:3-4

Recently my husband and I spent one Saturday working at a local soup kitchen. Although he had served there many times, this was my first time volunteering. I was assigned to be a kitchen worker, helping prepare a hearty lunch of soup, pasta, mixed vegetables, garlic bread, and dessert. The kitchen was a good vantage point for watching the dining hall volunteers relate to those who came for lunch. I noticed that the diners were referred to as guests, not the poor or homeless, but the guests. I watched several friendly women offer coffee and snacks to those who arrived early (some came on that cold winter morning two hours before serving actually began). The women greeted the guests as they might old friends, asking if they were keeping warm, did they need a heavier coat, could they use some bus tokens, had they been to the clinic to see about that cough? During lunch the dining room volunteers mingled with the guests, offering refills on drinks, second servings of pasta, and making sure each diner had a delicious looking dessert of their choice. There was no condescension, only sincere camaraderie and care. The volunteers lived out Philippians 2:3-4 and did not regard themselves better than the guests. They clearly enjoyed looking to the interests of others.

> *There was no condescension, only sincere camaraderie and care*

The morning we volunteered was New Year's Day, and I was humbled to begin a new year with these three reminders: I am very fortunate to have plenty to eat; I need to renew my personal calling to be a servant; and the interests of others are at least as important as my own.

prayer » Help me regard others as better than myself. I'll need help with that, God. In the name of Jesus, Amen.

Serve out of gratitude

Serve [the Lord] faithfully with all your heart; for consider what great things [God] has done for you. « 1 Samuel 12:24

I did not grow up in a wealthy family, but we had a large, warm house to live in and enough food to eat and clothing to wear. (I must admit, though, that while I had enough clothes to wear, I longed for my friends' more stylish and name-brand clothes. My mother either sewed my clothes or purchased them from a local low-budget store.)

A smile replaced her confusion, and she eagerly invited us inside

As a tangible expression of gratitude for what we had, my parents planned a charitable Christmas project each year. I most vividly remember the year Mom and Dad decided that we would spend much less on gifts for each other and use the extra money to "adopt" a family in the community. I would like to say we children thought this was a great idea and therefore didn't grumble about fewer gifts for ourselves, but that would be untrue. However, as we shopped for groceries, clothes, and toys for the family, we became more and more excited about the project. We made triple batches of our favorite Christmas cookies to share. Dad and I made a variety of handmade candles for the family, and my mother made extra of her famous caramels and peanut brittle.

On Christmas Eve morning, we filled three large boxes with food, clothes, and gifts, loaded them into the car, and drove to the family's house. When the young mother came to the door and saw all that we carried, she was confused. "These are for you," my mother said. Slowly a smile replaced her confusion, and she eagerly invited us inside to meet her children.

It's been a long time since that Christmas Eve delivery, but I have not forgotten the experience. I am grateful for parents who "served the Lord faithfully with their whole hearts" and for teaching me the importance of serving others out of gratitude for the great things God has done.

prayer » Great are you, Lord! Let me serve you faithfully and gratefully with my whole heart. In the name of Jesus, both Master and Servant, Amen.

Use your gifts

Like good stewards of the manifold grace of God, serve one another with whatever gift each of you has received.
« 1 Peter 4:10

In the Bible we read that there are a variety of abilities given to Christians. Some of these "spiritual gifts" include prophecy, ministry, teaching, encouragement, generous giving, hospitality, compassion, wisdom, discernment, and healing.[10] In today's Scripture we read that we are to serve each other with whatever gift we have received.

We can discover what kind of service we are gifted for and go from there

Your giftedness may not neatly correspond to the biblical lists, but you certainly have gifts. Identifying them is a first step in following Jesus faithfully. Serving others with those gifts is a second step. Although there are many good resources available to determine specifically what your spiritual gifts are, you probably have a pretty good idea what they are and how to use them to serve others. If not, ask yourself these questions: What things are you good at? What things do you do that make you happy? What kind of service excites you? What kind of service comes naturally to you? How could you mesh what you are good at and what makes you happy with serving others?

In the book of Acts, Peter and the other apostles, busy with their preaching and teaching, recognize that they have neither the time nor energy to appropriately care for the church's new converts. They appoint people who specifically have the gifts of hospitality and compassion to help attend to the needs of the church.[11] We, too, cannot serve everyone in every way, but we can discover what kind of service we are particularly gifted for and go from there—full speed ahead!

prayer » Help me discern what my spiritual gifts are so that I may faithfully serve you with grace and joy. Amen.

Serve Jesus by serving "the least of these"

Truly I tell you, just as you did it to one of the least of these who are members of my family, you did it to me.
« Matthew 25:40

Jesus tells his followers that when they take care of the hungry, thirsty, lonely, and sick people around them, they are actually doing these things for him.[12] In 1885, the Russian writer Leo Tolstoy wrote a short story called "Where Love Is, God Is." This story illustrates well what Jesus means in Matthew 25. There are many adaptations of this story, but this is a synopsis of the one I like best:

One night, God tells Martin, an old Russian shoemaker, that Jesus will be coming for a visit the next day. In the morning, an excited Martin runs to the window, eager to receive his holy guest. He doesn't see Jesus, but instead he notices a tired old man limping slowly down the street. Martin invites him inside to rest and have a cup of tea.

After the old man is on his way, Martin returns to the window to once again watch for Jesus, but sees only a young mother and her baby shivering in the cold. He calls for them to come sit by his fire while he finds a warm coat for the woman and a blanket for the baby.

Jesus did visit—not once but three times

After the pair leaves, Martin again watches for Jesus and notices a young boy slip an apple into his pocket from the nearby fruit stand. The shopkeeper, knowing that the boy did not pay for the apple, runs after him with a big stick. Martin hurries outside, intercepts the shopkeeper, and pays for the hungry boy's apple.

At the end of the day, Martin is still staring out the window, still waiting for Jesus. He asks God for an explanation of why Jesus never visited as promised. God replies that Jesus did visit—not once but three times.[13] Just as you serve one of the least of those who are members of God's family, you serve Jesus himself!

prayer » **In your name, Jesus, I want to serve others unselfishly and with joy. Because you love me, I will serve others. Amen.**

Living it out

Whoever serves me must follow me, and where I am, there will my servant be also. Whoever serves me, the Father will honor. « John 12:26

Explore interesting service opportunities in your local area. Here are a few suggestions to get you started:

- Google volunteer opportunities in your community.
- Talk to family and friends about people or places to serve.
- Ask your school guidance counselor for suggestions of places to volunteer.
- Visit your local library and have the reference librarian help you research possible service opportunities.
- Join a service organization such as Interact or Key Club at your school.
- Check with the staff of your congregation to see if there are things that need to be done around the church.
- Check with the staff of your church and ask them to share with you some of the community needs that have come to their attention.
- Look around your neighborhood. Are there people who need assistance with yard work, shopping, or household chores?
- Find places or organizations that need donations of food, baked goods, clothes, crafts, toys, etc., and formulate a plan to gather those things.
- If you knit or crochet, find information about charitable knitting or crocheting.
- Become involved in community garden projects.
- Find out about volunteer tutoring or childcare opportunities.

Be sure to add your own ideas to the list, and once you have done so, choose the five volunteer opportunities that interest you the most and best suit your gifts. Write each possibility on its own index card. Carefully think about each opportunity. How much time would it involve? Do you have the time it would take to serve well? What about transportation? What about your skill level for this service? Do any of the five opportunities seem too difficult, impractical, or overwhelming? Do any of them particularly excite you more than the others? How would your parents feel about this service? Is this something you have thought about before or is it an entirely new idea? Does the service opportunity involve any money, and if so, are you able to come up with the expense?

After answering the questions about the five volunteer opportunities, narrow the list down to three index cards. Talk to your family or other trusted adults about your choices and get their feedback on your ideas, on the organizations involved, and about your skill set.

Once you have received feedback, pray about these service opportunities for several days. After time to reflect and pray, choose the one that you want to explore and make a plan to get started.

The service opportunity I am going to explore is

_____

_____

_____

_____

_____

_____

_____

_____

_____

_____

I will get started by taking the following steps:

_____

_____

_____

_____

_____

_____

_____

_____

_____

_____

Jesus says that whoever serves him, God honors. God will surely bless your work and your good intentions. Prepare to gain much from serving others—maybe more than they will gain from you. It's amazing how that almost always happens. Now, go for it!

NOTES

1. Matthew 25:31-46 (my paraphrase)
2. Matthew 5:39
3. Matthew 5:44
4. Matthew 7:1-5
5. John 13:1-20
6. Luke 19:1-10
7. Luke 21:1-4
8. Mark 10:14-15
9. Luke 16:19-25
10. Romans 12:1-8; 1 Corinthians 12:4-11, 27-30; and Ephesians 4:7-13
11. Acts 6:1-7
12. Matthew 25:31-46
13. Masahiro Kasuya, Yoko Watari, Mildred Schell, and Leo Tolstoy, *The Shoemaker's Dream* (Valley Forge, PA: Judson Press, 1980).

ABOUT THE AUTHOR

Cindy Massanari Breeze has worked with children and youth her entire adult life, first as a public school music teacher and later as an associate pastor. A native of central Illinois, Cindy graduated from the University of Illinois in Urbana with a degree in music education and later earned a Certificate of Theological Studies from Associated Mennonite Biblical Seminary. One of her greatest joys in ministry was teaching the high school Sunday school class at First Mennonite Church in Urbana, for seventeen years.

Cindy and her husband, Clark, reside in Champagne, Illinois. They are parents to two adult daughters and grandparents to six grandchildren. Retired from pastoral ministry, Cindy is a hospice volunteer and enjoys spending time with Clark at their cabin in the woods, reading, knitting, and being with teenagers. She has written and directed four full-length musicals for young people and published several articles. This is her first book.

ACKNOWLEDGEMENTS

The idea for this book came from the youth who were in my Sunday school class: Mason Anders, Petey Biddle, Alexandra Bidner, Samuel Flannigan, Raina Liechty Martens, Ella Lubienski, Lucas Matthews, Michelle Moyer, Soren Rasmussen, Grace Sancken, Chloe Schreiber, Sophie Otto Shenk, Sarah Sutter, and Ben Zehr. It has been a pleasure to write about the topics you suggested. I am filled with gratitude to you and to all those who found their way into my classes and my heart over the years. I learned so much from each of you.

I would like to thank the readers—youth and adult—who read the manuscript and offered invaluable insight: Petey Biddle, Alexandra Bidner, Sheryl Dyck, Pastor Michael Crosby, Michelle Moyer, Carrie Nelson, Holly Nelson, Elizabeth Nisly-Nagele, Rosalee Otto, Jason Rhodes, Reuben Sancken, Dan Schreiber, and Sarah Sutter. This is a better book for your comments and corrections.

Thanks very much to my editor at MennoMedia, Byron Rempel-Burkholder. I am indebted to his keen eye, quick mind, and patient guidance.

Lastly, I honor each person in my family, especially those who made their way unwittingly into these pages. Much love to my parents, Joe and Francis, and Clark, Lara, Hilary, Steve, Jason, Anya, Dylan, Noah, Evan, Nora, Dominick, Tim, and Greg. All of you have inspired me, challenged me, and loved me. Thank you.

Cindy Massanari Breeze